THE STATUS BOOK

GARY BLAKE

THE STATUS BOOK

Illustrations by Nicky Zann

A Dolphin Book
Doubleday & Company, Inc.
Garden City, New York
1978

Library of Congress Cataloging in Publication Data
Blake, Gary.
The status book.
(A Dolphin book)
1. Social status—Anecdotes, facetiae, satire, etc.
I. Title.
PN6231.S633B55   031'.02
ISBN 0-385-13549-1
Library of Congress Catalog Card Number 77–94863

For Eve

CONTENTS

How Would You Like To . . .

ARTS AND ENTERTAINMENT

CLUBS AND ASSOCIATIONS

THE STATUS BOOK

DISTINCTIONS

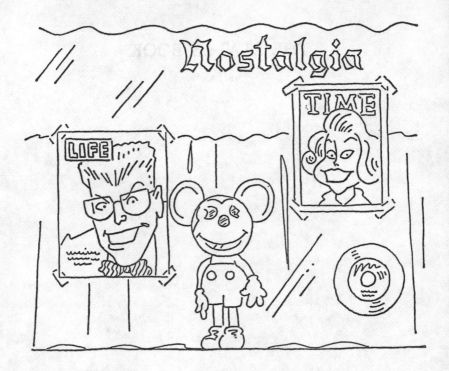

Have Your Biographical Sketch in Who's Who in America _____

Since the turn of the century Who's Who in America has separated the knowns from the unknowns in American art, business, politics, sports, public affairs, religion, and education. The 1977–78 edition (2,646 pp., $63.50) contains more than 72,000 full sketches of American notables, or only about 3 out of 10,000 Americans. You cannot beg, buy, or steal your way into the pages of Who's Who: it's strictly "Don't ask us, we'll ask you."

According to the standards of admission, the extent of an individual's "reference interest" is the sine qua non for determining who is to be included. Your reference interest is judged either on the position of responsibility you hold or on the level of significant achievement attained in your "career of meritorious activity." The President, his Cabinet, all federal judges, state governors, chief ecclesiastics, major business leaders are virtually assured of inclusion, but that still leaves plenty of space for up-and-coming biographees.

Recognition based on individual achievement is decided by a judicious process of evaluating qualitative factors. To be selected on this basis, you must have accomplished some conspicuous achievement like winning a Gold Medal at the Olympics or something that distinguishes you from the vast majority of your contemporaries (e.g., directing a Broadway hit, discovering a new galaxy, or giving birth to sextuplets).

Who's Who has a staff of stringers who scout new candidates and funnel your name to the Chicago office. You'll be sent a preliminary questionnaire that ferrets out the chief contributions among your diverse professional activities. It includes questions about your background, marital status, home, children, publications, honors, birthplace, how many lumps of sugar you take in your coffee, and other relevant details. Then a committee reviews your credentials. If you're accepted you'll be in Who's Who along with John Chancellor, Hank Aaron, H. R. Haldeman, Johnny Carson, Roy Rogers, Eldridge Cleaver, and Bob Dylan.

If your status is regional instead of national, you may well qualify for one of the other Who's Who volumes published annually by Marquis Who's Who: Who's Who in the East, Who's Who in the West, Who's Who in the Midwest, and so forth. If you are passed over by Who's Who, take solace in Groucho Marx's sentiment: "I wouldn't want to join any club that would have me as one of its members."

Appear on Eleanor Lambert's International Best-dressed List————————

Every December several judges sit down in a Manhattan office for one afternoon and determine which women will be recognized as the twelve Best-dressed Women of the Year. Usually eight judges hash things out, with the Holy Alliance of Eleanor Lambert and Eugenia Sheppard playing active parts in each selection. As they huddle together they begin the monumental task of whittling down the list Ms. Lambert has culled from suggestions sent in by over 2,000 fashion editors and observers of the international scene from all over the world. Models, designers, fashion writers are not eligible for the list. Other regulations are the prerogatives of Ms. Lambert, a fashion publicist and syndicated columnist, who has co-ordinated the List since 1940.

Among recent listees are an American TV star, the wife of a literary agent, an English aristocrat, the wife of a Venezuelan real estate mogul, a sculptor, and a Houston socialite. Past "best-dressed" women have included Mrs. Ronald Reagan, Lauren Bacall, Charlotte Ford, and Faye Dunaway.

If you were a fly on the wall at the Lambert meeting you'd find that Eugenia Sheppard wields pivotal influence although one major put-down from any of the judges makes a candidate's name disappear faster than the miniskirt. One way to guarantee not making the list is to want to be on it. One lady sent ninety post cards to Eugenia Sheppard telling what she wore each day. She never had a chance.

A big budget for clothes won't earn you a niche, but it doesn't hurt. Wearing too many jewels is considered "showy"; wearing too few may arouse pity. If you are showy, flashy, or just an easy target, you may well make Earl Blackwell's list of Worst-Dressed Women, which takes annual sideswipes at Zsa Zsa, Liz, Jackie, and Charo.

By virtue of uninhibited give-and-take, the Lambert List is eventually whittled to twenty-five names, and the ones that remain when the final twelve are chosen are usually those whose chief attribute was that they had the most vocal backers. The list is released in January. In 1977, Louise Nevelson, the seventy-seven-year-old sculptor, made the list wearing an outfit that matched a coat made from an old paisley shawl with a leather belt and a necklace. "Every time I put on clothes," Nevelson once wrote, "I am creating a picture, a living picture of myself." It is just this type of "originality" in dress that is likely to gain the attention of those who choose the best- and worst-dressed women of the world. Don't be surprised if you make both lists simultaneously. That's the fashion biz.

Have Your Achievement Recorded in The Guinness Book of World Records ⸺

Whether you wish to break the monotony of small-town life or just be "different," competing for a Guinness record is a sure-fire attention-getter. Before you start guzzling gallons of 7-Up, or

linking a seven-mile chain of paper clips, be careful! Record holders have already staked out territories such as baby carriage pushing, hula hoop twirling, apple peeling, rolling pin throwing, continuous clapping, grave digging, and most times hit by lightning.

Ever since Ross and Norris McWhirter first published the record book in 1956, compulsives of all descriptions have set their sights on being cited in it. In order to qualify for a mention in the next edition, your record must be legal, moral, and performed in the presence of news media or respected members of the community (not friends or relatives). Ask several witnesses to sign affidavits and keep a log testifying to "unremitting surveillance" of your deed. Take all of this verification (along with any news clippings of the record-setting) and mail it to General Editor, Guinness Superlatives Ltd., 2 Cecil Court, Enfield, Middlesex, England.

It is easier to gain status in the eyes of *Guinness* Book editors by beating an established record than by creating a new category or event. Politesse dictates that when you are about to improve on a record you invite a Guinness representative to observe you in action. They probably won't send anyone, but it's a nice gesture to ask them anyway. They'll decide whether your record is worthy of inclusion and will advise you whether you have sent sufficient documentation. If your feat is, literally, one for the books, you'll be sent a certificate by the Guinness people. It's a snap: just do something like . . . leapfrog for a distance of a hundred miles, or do 3,000 one-armed push-ups, or eat six pounds of shrimp at one sitting.

Sit at the Captain's Table Aboard the Queen Elizabeth II _____

If you've ever been on a cruise you know that some of your enjoyment depend on the quality of the table companions with whom you'll break bread three times a day. If you're traveling first class and are stuck with three disconsolate spinsters, a recent widow, and a teen-ager suffering from *anorexia nervosa,* your dream cruise may well turn into a nightmare. Aboard the *Queen Elizabeth II* the captain's table is the most highly coveted spot and when a person is invited to sit there he is permitted to share his every meal with the captain and other honored guests. But, with practically everyone aboard ship being a "somebody," how do they choose who gets to eat with the head man?

The captain decides. Requests are submitted to him from a variety of sources. A travel agent may whisper to his Cunard representative that an eminent author or internationally acclaimed film director will be traveling on a particular cruise, and wish to dine with the captain. *QE II* "repeaters" will also be given special consideration, since they may well have befriended the captain by this time. Other people come highly recommended by top executives at Cunard itself or by the ship's hotel manager (a rank that combines purser and chief steward), who may find among the passenger list—first class, not tourist—a scintillating somebody sure to "fit in."

If you do not get an invitation to sit at the captain's table it doesn't mean that you're being snubbed or should cable your psychiatrist, or that you bear the mark of an undeveloped territorial imperative. There are always 4 pools, 9 bars, 4 night clubs, and a 25,000-bottle wine cellar aboard this floating *fête champêtre* to soothe your ego. Sit with one other couple or dine alone, but anywhere you sit the waiters will find you and so will all those seven-course breakfasts and dinners.

Receive a Diploma from Le Cordon Bleu Cooking and Pastry School (Paris) ──────────

Just as margarine is no substitute for butter, no imitator matches the long-standing reputation for excellence of Le Cordon Bleu Cooking and Pastry School. Cordon Bleu won't just teach you esoteric ways of using truffles, it'll give you a disciplined approach to preparing and serving food. It'll make your dinner parties the envy of all. Also the *Grand Diplôme* will look great over the sink.

If you want that sheepskin, get ready to pack yourself off to Paris, attend classes faithfully, successfully complete examinations, and pay handsomely. In 1949, Julia Child attended the school (at the urging of her husband) and learned the essence of French cooking. Who knows what it will do for you? You must first make up your mind which diploma to strive for:

1. *Certificat Élémentaire* (Cooking or Pastry) received at completion of one or two terms.

2. *Diplôme de l'Année* (Cooking) received at the completion of three terms.

3. *Grand Diplôme* (Cooking) received at the end of four terms.

Each "term" runs approximately two months. Each week students are required to attend both practical classes as well as cooking demonstrations. The number of hours you spend in class will depend upon the particular course you choose (Cooking, Pastry, a combination of the two, or an advanced course), and the fees range from 2,900 francs ($580) for a six-week cooking course to about 8,700 francs ($1,740) for a twelve-week combination course.

Now, if you're still interested in matriculating, you must com-

plete an enrollment card, return it to the school with your photograph, and send a deposit of approximately a third of the
amount of the cost of your first term and 400 francs for each
further term. The balance is due at the beginning of each term.
In case of cancellation the deposit will not be refunded. No reduction will be allowed in case of absence. And there are no
doggy bags. . . .

Some more things you should know: an apron, a smock, and
three dish towels are required for the practical classes and are to
be purchased at the school.

An insurance policy must be subscribed to at Le Cordon Bleu;
it covers students in case of accident during the classes. The
school does not provide lodging for students but can send a list of
suggested hotels and pensions.

Courses generally are given (in French) from early January to
late March, late March to early July, early July to mid-August,
mid-August to mid-September and from mid-September to late
December. As at any other school, students will be tested at the
end of each term, so don't sign up if you're afraid of being
grilled.

However, if you'd prefer to study to be a headwaiter, the
schooling is much simpler. On the first day you learn how to say
"Your table should be ready in fifteen minutes. Would you care
to wait at the bar?" The next day is graduation.

Get a Place on the F.B.I.'s
"Ten Most Wanted Fugitives" List _____

QUESTION: Who is 5 feet 10 inches tall, weighs 166 pounds, is 37
years old, and has a lengthy criminal record sprinkled with violence? ANSWER: the average F.B.I. "Top Ten" fugitive.

The F.B.I.'s listing of fugitives, which began on March 14,
1950, with the co-operation of the American press, has proven to

be an ingenious way to catch a thief, or any other criminal for that matter. The phrase "Ten Most Wanted Fugitives" may be a lot less mellifluous than "Public Enemy No. 1," but it has proved more efficient in alerting the public at large about criminals at large.

Indicative of the achievements of this program is the box score of "Top Ten" captures, which has already totaled 315. Everyday citizens have directly aided in providing valuable information leading to the capture of 104 of these 315 criminals. Eliot Ness shouldn't get *all* the credit.

The time-honored criteria for selecting a candidate for this dishonors list include, in addition to current serious crime charges, a long history of vicious and violent criminal behavior of such a degree that the fugitive is considered a menace to society. The name of each of the criminals selected to be added to the "Ten Most Wanted Fugitives" list is given final personal approval by the director of the F.B.I. Patty Hearst didn't make the list because she already had a lot of publicity. New York's "Son of Sam" killer didn't appear on it because he had not been identified prior to capture.

If you do happen to be so unfortunate as to make this list, get ready for lots of free publicity: your photograph is assured of a place of honor at each F.B.I. office, police station, and post office in the United States. You'll also see your picture in the newspapers and on TV while you're in the slammer, because that's where you're almost sure to wind up. The average "Top Ten" fugitive spends an average of only 159 days on the list before he's captured. Or shot.

Become Imperial Wizard of the Ku Klux Klan

The first K.K.K. den was organized in Pulaski, Tennessee, in 1865. Its original name was Ku Kloi (from the Greek *Kyklos* meaning "circle" or "band"), and the group soon became known as the Klan, whereupon, during Reconstruction, it raised racism to an art form.

To become Imperial Wizard involves an elaborate process of primaries and elections that is detailed in their Constitution. It would be difficult to explain the process briefly because Klan terminology is strange to the non-Klan ear. The national organization is subdivided into Realms (states), Provinces (congressional districts), and Klaverns (local meeting places).

Now here's where things get difficult. The Imperial Wizard and his ten Genii run the Klan (the Genii include a Klaliff, a Klokard, a Kludd, a Kligrapp, a Klabee, a Kladd, Klorogo, Klexter, Knight Hawk, and Klonsuls). Beneath them is the Klan Bureau of Investigation, and beneath them are the Grand Dragons (state leaders) and their Hydras (advisers) and Kleagles (recruiters). At the Province level, the Grand Titan administers the established clubs and is aided by seven Furies (board of directors). At the Klavern level, the Exalted Cyclops (president of local club) governs with the aid of his twelve Terrors (includes all officers).

Most Klan meetings occur at night when cameras don't work so well and when sheets seem their whitest. But sometimes the Klan invites publicity, taking out radio spots and billboards in the South. In March 1977, David Duke, the twenty-six-year-old Grand Dragon of Louisiana, asked ABC television for "equal time" to respond to ABC's presentation of *Roots*.

The Klan claims to have members in every state in the union (Indiana has the most Klansmen), and all look to the Imperial

Wizard to direct the political, educational, and other activities of the Klan. There is even an elaborate plan of succession, should the Imperial Wizard die or become incapacitated.

It doesn't seem to be very rewarding to be Imperial Wizard when so much of the time you're under wraps, but there are a number of Grand Dragons across America who'd love to direct the Klan. A Klansman would probably advise them to be patient (keep their sheets on), and burn that cross when they come to it.

Woody Allen said it best. He tells a story of traveling through the South and meeting up with several Klansmen. Finally he saw the leader. "I knew he was the leader," said Woody, "because he was wearing contour sheets."

Join the Communist Party

You've heard about card-carrying Communists, and now you've decided to be one of Marx's brothers and change the system from the outside. The Party is a somewhat seductive status symbol for anyone who has ever dabbled in left-wing politics.

If you write to the headquarters of the Communist Party of the United States of America, you will probably receive some literature, a copy of their Constitution, and an application to join. The form letter expresses the hope that you will become convinced that the Communist Party, U.S.A., is the party with the policies, theory, organization, and membership needed to play a special role in helping win fundamental social changes for the better. After receiving your application, they will write you about the next step.

The Communist Party application form asks a few simple questions about your age, occupation, address, and phone number. One might easily assume that everyone who fills out the application blank automatically becomes a Party member. Not so. The "second step" is usually your being approached by a Party member who'll sound you out about your political ideas and your personal life. The Party wants no part of you if you're an alcoholic, a crackpot, or some type of jejune Jacobin. The Party is looking for serious-minded men and women who understand and accept the theories of Marx, Engels, and Lenin, and who see the application of those theories to the American political and social system. In fact, years ago, one needed a set of impeccable credentials as a radical before the Communists would even consider you for Party membership.

According to the Party Constitution, membership is open to "any resident of the United States, 18 years of age or over . . . who subscribes to the principles and purposes of the Communist Party." He must also be endorsed by at least two Party members, and his application shall be subject to approval by a majority vote of the club to which the applicant is presented. There is always a lingering fear that, although Americans are free to join any political party we wish, Big Brother will watch us if we join the Communist Party. True, the F.B.I. may start a file on you, but so what? You can keep one on them.

Sit on New York's Grand Jury ─────────────

Being summoned for jury duty often means spending an eternity in the jurors' room waiting to be assigned to a case, or sitting through a case wherein lackadaisical lawyers contest the mundane misdemeanors of their clients. The grand jury is different: prestigious, privileged, and privy to important cases presented in a more concise manner than that of regular courtroom trials.

The secrecy that surrounds grand jury meetings not only protects the names of grand jurors but also encourages witnesses to testify without fear of retaliation and protects the independence of the grand jury. Secrecy also protects the reputation of those whom the grand jury does not indict. Hundreds of thousands of

New Yorkers are destined to be petty jurors, but only a select few thousand get to be grand jurors. Why be petty when you could be grand?

For openers: you must be an American citizen, between the ages of eighteen and seventy, intelligent, well spoken, well read, never involved in a misdemeanor of moral turpitude and never convicted of a felony. Each year, grand jurors are selected from names on voting lists and income tax mailing lists. However, if you're eager to volunteer, go to the Jury Division (100 Centre Street, New York) and let them know you're available. Saturnine civil servants will ask you why you're volunteering, because they're not interested in gadflies out to "get someone."

If your application is accepted, you'll be fingerprinted, and your fingerprints will be sent to the state capital where they'll be used to uncover any police record a prospective juror may have neglected to mention. The county Jury Board operates similarly to a draft board in that it makes its final selection based on how many jurors are needed. Once you are selected for the grand jury, you may be summoned, at random, to serve in any given month. You will report to Part 30 (in New York, all courtrooms are called "Parts"), 100 Centre Street, usually on the first Monday of the month, and be empaneled on one of four or five juries, each containing twenty-three people.

From then on, your job will be to listen to the prosecutor present evidence, hear the interrogation of witnesses, determine whether a crime has been committed, and then determine whether a particular person is likely to have committed it.

If most of the grand jurors believe a particular person is responsible for the crime, they'll vote for an indictment. An indictment is only a formal accusation, a charge on which the grand jury recommends the accused should be tried. It is not a conviction, nor does it determine the defendant's guilt or innocence. Someone else does *that*. Try to look intelligent, dress neatly, and stay about as silent as the *c* in "indictment." Keep your eyes and your mind open, and you'll make a very grand juror indeed.

Your close friends will probably find out that you've been chosen to serve on the grand jury, and they'll be anxious to know all the details of important, upcoming investigations. Then you will be able to exercise the privilege of answering each of their questions with a weighty sigh, a profound turn of the head, and the whispered, tactful rejoinder: "I'm not at liberty to discuss it."

Have Your Daughter Become a Debutante ———

How does it feel to be a debutante and formally take your place in society in an evening of pomp and circumstance? Any deb will tell you it's a ball. Debutantes are America's answer to princesses, and their coming-out parties trumpet their formal entry into a world of elegance, charitable deeds, responsibility, and social leadership.

If you are what is known as "old money" (i.e., you do not find it necessary to cash your pay check on the same day you receive it), you may wish to have your daughter come out at your own home, yacht club, or private island. Henry Ford II's daughter Anne had her debut at the family digs. In fact, Ford built two large guesthouses on his property solely to accommodate the serving of his guests on that occasion, and the actual debut was made in his private ballroom. What? You don't have a private ballroom in your home?

Let's add up some of the possible expenses you'll incur in the process of grooming your daughter to be a debutante:

You'll need a part-time social secretary, someone to snap your photo at the right function (cost: let's say $3,000 a year for two years). Find a fashionable private school like Foxcroft, a nice college like Mount Holyoke or Radcliffe ($25,000 minimum for the college education). Other expenses include a nice tea ($1,000) to show the cut of your jib, and a wardrobe ($5,000 a year) that doesn't come from a thrift shop.

As for the debut itself, why not go the whole hog and have it at the International Debutantes' Ball in New York (assuming you can rustle up a sponsor and five letters of recommendation from people willing to testify to your daughter's good character)? Presentation fees are $1,000; $300 for the ticket plus escort (also there's a military escort who escorts your daughter and her escort). Tickets for guests are $100 each.

You should be able to keep the whole socialization process under $50,000 including white gloves and wrist corsages. But if you're strapped, or if your "old money" has begun to decompose, or if the whole thing sounds like a terrible bother, simply don't have a debut. Now *that's "chic."*

HONORS

See Your Face on an American Postage Stamp

In 1847 the first adhesive postage stamp in America was issued, and it sported a picture of that jack-of-all-trades, Ben Franklin. But it wasn't until 1893 that the Post Office decided to initiate a Commemorative Stamp Program as a way of reminding America about its history and achievements. Since then the Postmaster General has determined who and what appears on those stamps.

A Citizens' Advisory Committee was set up in 1971 because the Postmaster General was overloaded with requests to have particular people and events on the commemorative stamps. You see, the Advisory Committee receives about 4,000 letters a year, suggesting everything from a stamp commemorating Hank Aaron's lifetime home run record to one commemorating two hundred years of Impeachable Offenses. The fourteen individuals who comprise the committee—historians, stamp collectors, Post Office officials—meet four times a year, research each of the suggestions, and then turn over their recommendations to the Postmaster General.

The only absolute criterion for being honored on a commemorative stamp is that the person being honored has to have been dead for at least ten years by the time his stamp is issued. Perhaps if you were a President, they'd bend this rule for you. Stamps may commemorate great athletes, scientists, writers, businessmen, or statesmen. If stamps are designed to commemorate an event (such as the fiftieth anniversary of Lindbergh's solo crossing of the Atlantic or Project Mercury or the sesquicentennial of the Erie Canal), they are usually issued on the exact anniversary of the historical event.

So, if you have someone or some event in mind, get your suggestions in to the committee in plenty of time to allow a well-timed release of the stamp. Remember that the wheels of progress grind slowly at the Post Office and that it takes several months—or even years—for a stamp to be designed, plates to be made, and for the stamp to be printed. You can read about past commemorative stamps in a small book entitled *Stamps and Stories,* available at many large post offices in the United States.

If you ever do have your face on a stamp, your descendants can buy it on the first day of issue at some appropriate local post office (such as the one in your home town or the town of your birth). After the first issue, most post offices around the country will have at least a few of "your" stamps in stock. In case the supply runs short—and since the average run is about 130,000,000, it is doubtful that will happen—your friends and loved ones can always write to the Post Office in Washington for more. And with so many free-lance philatelists giving you the stamp of approval, you'll surely gain immortality as a man of letters.

Earn Sainthood in the Catholic Church ————

If one sometimes thinks of himself as a "saint" his friends and followers can make it official by reporting his saintly deeds to the Church and helping to see that, after losing his temporals, he becomes venerated as a saint.

The initial step—a formal inquiry known as the Ordinary Process—is instituted by the diocese in which the prospective saint lived. The inquiry is conducted by three judges, a notary, and a "promoter of the faith" (commonly called "devil's advocate") who eventually presents the flaws and weaknesses of the arguments for sainthood to the Sacred Congress in the Vatican. Rome's investigation determines whether a cult has already begun to form around the proposed saint. The Apostolic Process begins as the Sacred Congress investigates the reality and nature of the virtues and miracles ascribed to the person to be beatified. You should have two fully authentic miracles on your résumé if you expect to survive the Apostolic Process. Bishop John Neumann, who achieved sainthood in 1977, and who died at age forty-eight in 1860, had three miracles attributed to him, and in all three cases the cures he effected were "medically and scientifically inexplicable."

You don't become a saint overnight. It takes many years, and it happens in stages. Beatification is the first stage. At this stage, a declaration is made by the Pope that one of the faithful, because of a life of virtue or the heroic death of martyrdom, is entitled to be blessed. This permits veneration of the person only in those places where he or she lived or in the houses of the community that he or she founded. This is the final stage before ultimate canonization. During this phase a ceremony is held in St. Peter's and the decree of beatification is read. There is an unveiling of the picture of "The Blessed" above the chair of St. Peter; a *Te Deum* is sung in celebration of the newly beatified.

Finally, after more time has passed, the Pope presides over a meeting of cardinals and they hear a summary of the beatified's life (it took Bishop John Neumann's followers over eighty-four years to reach this step). After the summary is presented, the Pope asks, in Latin, "How does it seem?" Each cardinal then rises in turn, raises his red *zucchetto* (satin skullcap), and says *"Placet* [It pleases me]."

Since saints are dead long before they're canonized, they miss the short ceremony in which the Pope says their names and declares each to be "a Saint, and we inscribe his name in the Calandar of Saints and establish that he should be directly honored among the Saints in the universal church."

Be Elected to the French Academy _____

Founded in 1635 by Louis XIII and his chief minister, Cardinal Richelieu, the French Academy is the most famous literary society in the Western world. L'Académie Française is one of five organizations within the Institut de France (the other four are Inscriptions and Belles-Lettres, Sciences, Fine Arts, and Moral and

Political Sciences) and its purpose is to preserve the purity of the French language. The forty members of the Academy are known as "immortals" because of their deathless reputations. Once elected to the Academy, they are members for life.

Would you like to wear the traditional bicorne and cape signifying your membership in the Academy? You need to be French (Ionesco was actually born in Romania, but he's lived in France most of his life), have established fame, and have declared your eligibility for the Academy. There is an unwritten code of "personal respectability" and ethical behavior to which all members are supposed to adhere. They don't like troublemakers in the Academy, so rabble rousers like Rousseau, Flaubert, Balzac, Hugo, Molière, Stendhal, Rochefoucauld, and Proust found themselves blackballed for one reason or the other.

However, if you do get into the French Academy, you'll make friends with other members like René Clair (elected 1960) or Ionesco (elected 1970) and with non-literary members such as Claude Lévi-Strauss (1973).

If you don't make it, don't worry. Do you know how difficult it is to have a bicorne dry-cleaned?

Appear on the Queen's Honors List _____

It's always nice to get a pat on the back, but when that pat is administered by an English monarch's sword, it's your day to become a knight.

Knighthood and other honors are announced in one of two annual Honors Lists and are published in supplements to the London *Gazette,* one on January 2 and the other in June, on the day of the sovereign's official birthday. These lists name the people the sovereign has decided to honor and the specific honor conferred upon each. Special lists are also issued on such occasions as a coronation or jubilee, on the retirement of a govern-

ment because of a general election, or on the retirement of a
Prime Minister.

In choosing the listees, the Queen acts on the advice of the
Prime Minister, who may use any sources of information that
might be helpful. For example, government departments can
suggest both civil servants and members of the public for their
achievements in the sphere of activity for which the department
is responsible; and the Leader of the Opposition is consulted before members of the parliamentary opposition are selected for life
peerages. Certain honors are conferred by the personal selection
of the sovereign; these are the Order of the Garter, the Order of
the Thistle, the Order of Merit, and the Royal Victorian Order.

Simply stated, life peers are given the title "Lord" (e.g., Lord
Olivier), and they may not pass that title down to their heirs.
The Queen can also dub you a knight or a dame (e.g., Sir John
Betjeman or Dame May Whitty), but that title has less status
than that of peer.

Knights and dames of orders distinguish themselves every
time they write a letter, because their honor allows them the
privilege of adding the initials of their rank after their names.
For example, ranks of the Most Excellent Order of the British
Empire are: Knight or Dame Grand Cross (G.B.E.), Knight or
Dame Commander (C.B.E.), Officer (O.B.E.), and Member
(M.B.E.). P. G. Wodehouse was given the honor of knight commander of the Order of the British Empire. Other good knights
include Sir Richard Attenborough and Sir Freddie Laker. In
1965, the Beatles were made members of the Most Excellent
Order of the British Empire—a lower rank than knight.

As a safeguard to insure the integrity of these awards, a Political Honors Scrutiny Committee sees all proposals for honors for
political services and has the duty of reporting to the Prime
Minister any names it might consider unsuitable. In addition, it
is an offense, under the Honours (Prevention of Abuses) Act
1925, for anyone to offer to procure an honor for money or other
valuable consideration, or for anyone to give money or take other
action with the object of obtaining an honor.

Following the publication of the Honors List, investitures are
held at which recipients of honors receive from the Queen the

insignia of the honor. Knights receive the accolade (the touch of the sword), although knights may adopt the prefix "Sir" from the date of the official announcement of conferral of the honor. Put it on your letters, put it on your mailbox, put it on your sweater, if you care to—you've earned it.

Have an Airport Named After You _____

How would you like your name up in flights? Imagine telling a cab driver to take you to your own airport. Are you worthy of the honor? There's not much of a chance that you'll be so honored, but you could get lucky.

Airports are usually named after local politicians, former Presidents, reigning monarchs, or aviation pioneers. Each locality decides its own airport's name. The Port Authority of New York and New Jersey suggested that Idlewild Airport be renamed John F. Kennedy Airport and, during a few weeks in 1963, all those airport signs were changed and luggage tags began to use the "JFK" initials.

It might be interesting to find out a bit about the backgrounds of some people who have been so honored, so that you may profit from their examples. Mitchell Field in Milwaukee is named for a general, while Stapleton International in Denver is named for a former mayor of that city. O'Hare in Chicago is named for a Navy flier killed during World War II, but Lambert Field in St. Louis is named for the owner of a pharmaceutical firm who was active in aviation. Thomas Bell Love, for whom the Dallas airport is named, opposed Alfred E. Smith for the presidential nomination in 1928.

Occasionally an airport is named after a patriot (Patrick Henry Airport, Newport News, Virginia), an aviator (Lindbergh Field, San Diego), a world-famous humorist (Will Rogers World Airport, Oklahoma City), or former heads of state (Simon Bolivar, Caracas; David Ben-Gurion Airport, Tel Aviv).

Once in a while someone gets the idea to name an airport after a concept—Friendship International in Baltimore, for example—but even that name was changed because no one knew exactly where to find friendship. President Eisenhower suggested that the new airport serving Washington be named after John Foster Dulles, his Secretary of State. When John F. Kennedy became President he tried to undo Eisenhower's plan, but he was unsuccessful, hence Dulles International. Although political wheeling and dealing may help your chances, you could just be outstanding in your field (Da Vinci Airport, Rome), but whatever you do, don't get born with a name that's hard to spell. New Orleans' airport was named "Maupassant" and then renamed because nobody could spell the name correctly. If you don't wind up giving your name to your local airport, you can always buy some land, clear an air strip, and name it after yourself. Either that, or change your name to La Guardia.

Set Your Footprints in Cement at Mann's (Formerly Grauman's) Chinese Theatre ⸻

In the half century since Sid Grauman opened a movie palace on Hollywood Boulevard, three generations of film stars have left their footprints in Grauman's cement as well as in the sands of time.

Norma Talmadge was the first of hundreds of film stars who have cemented their immortality by stepping into the mysterious formula which includes glycerine, oil of peppermint, and sand. The origin of this custom is dubious. One apocryphal story has Grauman slipping off a builder's plank into the wet cement, thus hatching the idea of having film stars imprint various parts of their anatomy in cement. Mary Pickford claims that the tradition started when a pet dog left its prints. Although the origin is

dubious, the tradition caught on and has become a part of Hollywood history, despite the fact that the theatre is now known as
"Mann's Chinese," after the conglomerate that owns it.

Although he sold it to Twentieth Century-Fox just a few years
after building it, flamboyant, colorful Sid Grauman managed the
theatre until two years before he died. Another apocryphal story
—it seems Grauman's life was a series of such stories—tells of his
propensity for sleeping until noon every day. He refused all
phone calls until that hour. Like Nero fiddling while Rome
burned, Grauman snoozed while the Dow Jones plunged on October 29, 1929. By the time he got to the phone the market had
crashed and he was out $6,000,000.

In spite of his alleged mishaps, Grauman lived to see his
theatre prosper and become world-famous, and since then many
film stars such as Douglas Fairbanks, Mary Pickford, Doris Day,
Rock Hudson, Jane Russell, Marilyn Monroe, and Jack Nichol-
son have all waded in. If footprints all look alike to you, you
may also admire cement imprints of Joe E. Brown's mouth, Tom
Mix's horse, John Barrymore's profile, and Jimmy Durante's
schnoz. Among the non-humans represented are Rin-Tin-Tin
and the loveable *Star Wars* robots (See Threepio and Artoo Dee-
too) and its villain Darth Vader.

To be cast in cement, you must be more than just cast in a
film. You must have made a "contribution to the industry."
Today, a six-man committee of the Mann Corporation decides
just who fits into that category, and they meet once a year to decide just who gets stuck. However, in recent years few have been
so honored. It seems that the theatre is running out of space.

Maybe it is fitting that as Hollywood declines its traditions
fade. Besides, how could anyone compete with one starlet's
handprints, footprints, and message, set in 1929 when she was
twenty-two years old: "May this cement our friendship—Joan
Crawford"?

Earn the Honorary Title of Kentucky Colonel

Whether you're a Yankee or a Rebel, you can be an Honorary Kentucky Colonel and have a signed parchment certificate, with a seal and gold ribbon. You must be recommended to the governor for outstanding contributions to your community, state, or nation, or for some worthy endeavor or achievement. There have been a few governors of Kentucky who handed them out as freely as if they were campaign literature, but the governor's approval is all that's necessary for you to be presented with your certificate as a Kentucky Colonel.

The list of Kentucky Colonels resembles a Who's Who, including many men and women from foreign countries. The certificate with the signatures of the governor and secretary of state and the seal of the Commonwealth of Kentucky hangs on the wall of many distinguished government leaders, businessmen, and entertainers. Bing Crosby, Red Skeleton, John Glenn, Jr., who was commissioned while orbiting the earth, the late former President Lyndon B. Johnson, and the late English Prime Minister Winston Churchill are among many to have been honored with the rank of Kentucky Colonel.

It all began with the first governor of Kentucky, Isaac Shelby, who gave his son-in-law, Charles S. Todd, the title of colonel on his staff. Shelby later issued commissions to all who enlisted in his regiment in the War of 1812. Later governors commissioned colonels to act as their protective guard; they wore uniforms and were present at most official functions.

The Honorable Order of Kentucky Colonels, a society that all those who have been commissioned Kentucky Colonels are invited to join, was founded in 1932 by Governor Ruby Lafoon and has since been officially incorporated as a charitable organization. The governor and the lieutenant governor of Kentucky serve as commander-in-chief and deputy commander-in-chief respectively. All officers serve without remuneration.

Colonel Anna Friedman Goldman has been Secretary and keeper of the Seal since 1940 and her home—The Forest, Anchorage, Kentucky—is the national headquarters.

Get out there and do the Bluegrass State proud—perhaps they're chilling a mint julep with your name on it.

Win the Congressional Medal of Honor _____

If there's one medal that tests your mettle, it is the Congressional Medal of Honor. It is what the well-dressed heroes are wearing, and it is given to someone who distinguishes himself above and beyond the call of duty:

1. while engaged in an action against an enemy of the United States.
2. while engaged in military operations involving conflict with an opposing force; or
3. while serving with friendly forces engaged in an armed conflict against an opposing armed force in which the United States is not a belligerent party.

Approved by President Lincoln on July 12, 1862, the award was first presented by Secretary of War Stanton on March 25, 1863. On February 15, 1917, 911 names were removed from the Medal of Honor Roll by the Army Medal of Honor Board. The Board ruled that these 911 individuals had not performed acts of sufficient merit to earn this award.

It takes two to make a medal winner, so, when you are just about to capture an enemy battalion singlehanded, make sure that a friend is there to witness the event. In fact, you need at least two eyewitnesses. Remember that you can't count on captured enemy soldiers to put in a good word for you.

The deed must be so outstanding that it clearly distinguishes your gallantry beyond the call of duty and is above lesser forms of bravery; it must involve the risk of your life and be the type of deed which, if you had not done it, would not subject you to any justified criticism.

A recommendation for the Army or Air Force Medal of Honor must be made within three years of the date of the deed. The recommendation for a Navy Medal of Honor must be made within three years of the deed and awarded within five years.

Apart from the great honor it conveys, a Medal of Honor can, under certain conditions, allow its owner to obtain free military air transportation, a modest pension, and the privilege of wearing the medal on appropriate occasions.

Occasionally a Medal of Honor has been awarded by a special act of Congress—the first being in December 1927, honoring Captain Charles A. Lindbergh. So that increases your chances: either capture a batallion singlehanded *or* fly the Atlantic alone. . . .

Qualify for Burial at Arlington National Cemetery

Arlington National Cemetery is a nice place to visit but would you want to be buried there? If one were not already deceased, the hassle over qualifying for burial would probably be enough to make any soldier just fade away. If your heirs are status-conscious, here are a few of the things they'll need to know about Arlington's red tape.

The hallowed ground, contained within the 1,100-acre Arlington estate in Arlington, Virginia, was established in 1864. Title to the land was obtained in 1883 and cost taxpayers $150,000. To be buried at Arlington, you must be eligible, and that means having been active in high-level federal service, a recipient of the Medal of Honor (a Distinguished Service Cross, Distinguished

Service Medal, Silver Heart, or Purple Heart will also do), a Supreme Court justice, Chief of Staff, chief of the Foreign Service or an ambassador who was in the military. You can also get in if you are a retired member of the armed forces receiving pay or eligible to receive pay. Soldiers who fall in action are also eligible whether they fought in World War I, World War II, the Korean War, or Vietnam.

If you are eligible, your next of kin requests authority for burial from the superintendent of the cemetery. Families of soldiers who were on active duty at the time of death are required to supply a statement from the commanding officer; in the case of veterans, the Veterans' Administration is consulted. The interment section of the cemetery also checks to see if any relatives are eligible to be buried with you. A dishonorable discharge, even if you die in a V.A. hospital, makes you *persona non grata* at Arlington.

Arlington National Cemetery strives for maximum dignity and it succeeds. There is no charge for a grave or marker, and potted plants are the only foliage allowed at the grave. Burial is usually two or three days after death. By the way, there are no reservations; space is assigned at the time of death.

Become a Delegate to the Republican or Democratic National Convention _____

Hobnobbing with high-powered politicos can be just as exciting as seeing your favorite film stars in person. Why not attend a national political convention and do both? You'll get to wear a funny hat, make a lot of noise, and still be secure in the knowledge that you are doing your duty to both party and country. If you're lucky, you may see such statesmen as Shirley MacLaine, Warren Beatty, Efrem Zimbalist, Jr., and John Wayne right alongside you.

There's wide variation, state to state, on the regulations pertaining to delegate selection, but the three main selection processes take place at state primaries, at state conventions, and in state committees. Take the Republican Party as an example. In Alabama the primary system is used, and potential delegates file declarations of candidacy with the state chairman of the party. You have a good chance to be chosen; sometimes delegates go unchallenged. Commitment to a specific candidate is optional. Potential delegates' names appear on a ballot and are selected by party members eligible to vote in the primary. In Kansas you are selected by the state convention, after you've succeeded in being chosen at precinct, county, or congressional district level. Women stand a good chance in Kansas, because the state's Republican Party rules stipulate that the total number of delegates must be approximately equally divided among men and women. In Massachusetts selection of delegates occurs after the state primary when the state committee asks its divisions to nominate delegates. During this same period of time, task forces representing youth, the elderly, women, blacks, and other special interests caucus. These potential candidates for delegates then appear before the state committee to answer questions and indicate a preference for a candidate or willingness to be bound.

To find out exactly what the procedure is in your state, it's best to write to the state committee of the party of your choice. It helps if you are active on a local level, since so much of the decision making is done by those who have been active in politics all their lives. In many states the rules are that there are *no automatic delegates,* so don't assume that your state's delegates are sewed up years before the convention. Don't be afraid to enlist the aid of friends, cousins, aunts, and any members of clubs or organizations of which you are a member. You may find that, simply through persistence, you'll win a delegate's spot at the convention. You may do it because of your address, as a member of an obscure ethnic group, or because you happen to be elderly, but you can't tell how far you'll go in the party until you take this first step. Who knows: your vote may be the one that decides who'll be your party's standard-bearer, and perhaps the next President of the United States.

Enter the Miss America Contest _____

When you get to Atlantic City, your life will consist of seven judges judging, six parents fainting, five maids a-weeping, four twirles twirling, and a handshake from Bert Parks. But the nationally televised Miss America Pageant, held annually during Labor Day week, is the culmination of state and local competitions held throughout America.

A few of the major requirements for entering a local Miss America Preliminary are that you be female between the ages of seventeen and twenty-six, a high school graduate, single, an American citizen, have never been married or had a marriage annulled, and are of good moral character. Just entering the local contest usually gives a girl enough to talk about for the rest of the year. Your only expense is likely to be your wardrobe. You'll need a long evening gown, which need not be expensive, a swim suit, and a "talent" costume, assuming your particular talent requires one. Certainly a bright costume will look smashing as you play the New World Symphony on the tom-toms or do a rendition of "Moon River" on the glockenspiel. You need not have training in one of the performing arts to gain attention, because pageant audiences have cheered girls whose ingenuity has led them to dramatize their hobbies, interests, and future careers.

You will have an opportunity to meet the judges at an interview session and talk to them about your interests, while they size you up. Similar interviews are held as you progress to the state and national competitions.

The local pageant organization takes care of the expenses necessary for its winner to compete in the state pageant. At the state level, the competition is conducted in the same manner as was the local pageant. Then the state pageant committee assumes expenses for its winner to participate with the forty-nine other young ladies in Atlantic City. Guarding the honor of these fifty nubile lasses are official hostesses appointed by the Miss America Pageant.

Some last-minute advice: Don't try to be too sexy or wink at the judges. Don't talk about your plans to become a nudist or your admiration for Cher or Bert Parks's wet look. Don't burst into tears when you win (just *appear* to) because tears are hell on mascara.

Miss America gets to travel all around the country, being the center of attention wherever she goes, and just as one is a Phi Beta Kappa for life, so each winner can proudly refer to herself as a "former Miss America" whenever the subject comes up in conversation.

Become Homecoming Queen at a University —

Do you know what a homecoming queen is? She's the official symbol of homecoming, that's what. And what is "homecoming"? It is the name given to that special day or weekend when alumni come home to the alma mater, attend the homecoming football game, reminisce about their days as undergraduates, and get a beer at the local pub that used to ask them for I.D.s when they were undergraduates.

To be elected homecoming queen usually certifies for all time that you were both pretty and popular when you were an undergraduate. You can do some politicking for the post by being active in extracurricular activities, because various college organizations, fraternities, and sororities select candidates for homecoming queen. Then the whole student body votes for the candidates on the basis of beauty and talent. At Pittsburg State College in Kansas a homecoming candidate usually plays an instrument or recites something. The homecoming parade is October 15, and (at Pittsburg) the queen is chosen the night before. She represents the whole college and receives a football signed by all the players.

At the University of Wisconsin, homecoming is like Christmas, Easter, Mardi Gras, and Robert La Follette's birthday all rolled into one. Usually the fraternities take the lead in organizing the various activities, which include promoting the homecoming game (by erecting displays along Langdon Street, Wisconsin's fraternity row) and fussing over each candidate with interviews, electioneering, and elaborate parties. The Wisconsin Student Association appoints a committee to help carry out homecoming festivities and to stir up the homecoming spirit among both Greek and non-Greek factions of the campus.

The honor of being elected homecoming queen far outstrips that of being freshman queen, prom queen, queen of the junior carnival, or window monitor in grammar school, for not only are you a heroine to the student body but you have a chance to socialize with deans, vice-presidents, and even the president of the college. You get to sit on the fifty-yard line and cheer for the home team while a thirty-mile-per-hour wind freezes your smile and plays havoc with your hairdo.

Become a Playboy Bunny ───────────────

For the American male, Peter Rabbit, Bugs Bunny, the Easter Bunny, and Peter Cottontail all pale in comparison with that table-hopping mammal, the Playboy bunny. The natural habitat of the Playboy bunny is the Playboy Club, located in rural (e.g., Great Gorge, New Jersey; Lake Geneva, Wisconsin) as well as urban environments (Los Angeles, St. Louis, Tokyo, London). Many a lass has dreamed of donning the ears and tail of a Playboy bunny, not only because it marks her as having the allure characteristic of a Playboy centerfold, but also because the work pays well.

Regardless of your face and figure, you have the right to at least go through the Bunny Hunt, that semi-ritualistic audition

by which new Playboy bunnies are chosen. Simply call the local
Playboy Club and ask to speak to the Bunny Mother. She'll tell
you when the next group of girls is scheduled to audition. At
the New York Playboy Club (which employs about 120 bunnies,
more than any of the other clubs), your audition will take
place in front of the Bunny Mother, the Assistant Bunny Mother,
and the general manager of the club. Usually the hunt is scheduled for Friday afternoon, when about fifty lovely ladies assemble
at the service entrance of the club. Before the girls change into
their leotards or two-piece bathing suits, they wait downstairs,
assess the competition, and attract the stares of 59th Street stroll-
ers. The audition consists of little more than parading in front of
the judges and displaying your profile as well as front and rear
views. The girls, one at a time, then stand in front of the judges,
knees together, back to them, turn once more and give them a
big smile. Don't worry about your age. You should be old enough
to serve liquor, but you are not legally required to state your age.
Some bunnies are in their fifties!

Don't be surprised if the judges ask you questions during the
Bunny Hunt. "Have you applied before?" "Did anyone refer
you?" The judges simply want to see if you make conversation
easily. If they ask you whether you have any special qualifications, tell them that you can type sixty words a minute—you're
bound to get a big laugh.

The judges grade the girls from 1 to 4 (a composite rating,
with 4 being the worst score). Judgments are based on face,
figure, personality, and a certain "bunny quality" that Bunny
Mothers are reluctant to put into words. It has to do with the
clean, girl-next-door image that made *Playboy* models so special.
It does not have to do with overt sexiness, so leave the waist
bracelets, lace-up boots, false eyelashes, and fish-net stockings at
home.

If you are chosen to be a bunny you'll get to wear the costume
made up of cottontail, ears, as well as the cuffs, cuff links, bow
tie, and collar of a formal dress shirt. Your take-home pay will
consist of a low hourly salary but also a whopping 17½ per cent
tip added automatically to each check. If your service is excellent, you'll probably get tipped above the regular tip. In New

York, bunnies average $400 to $500 in salary and tips every week.

Being a bunny means more than money, it also means the likelihood of being approached to pose in the magazine. It means the opportunity to be selected Bunny of the Year, and to win all the 24-karat items that bunnies adore.

. . . or Queen of the Tournament of Roses ———

Since the Tournament of Roses parade is seen by an estimated world-wide television audience of over 125,000,000 people, it's no wonder that the competition for queen of the parade excites an intense fervor among Pasadena girls. Every girl between the ages of seventeen and twenty-one, single (never married), maintaining at least a C average can compete, assuming that she attends either public or parochial school, college or junior college in the Pasadena Area Community College District. This area of Southern California contains more than twenty-three schools. The competition used to be limited to just women attending Pasadena Junior College, but in 1968 the contest opened up to include all the neighborhood schools.

On the last Saturday in September, roughly 700 to 800 girls begin to be screened by a nine-person committee of judges known as the "Queen and Court Committee." These nine judges are selected from the more than 8,000 full-time workers on the Tournament of Roses who rotate on twenty-nine different committees. Each girl is interviewed for a few minutes, and each is known only by a number, not a name. If a judge should happen to recognize one of the girls, he is expected to disqualify himself from judging her.

Each week, for four weeks, girls are gradually eliminated, and eventually twenty-five finalists are selected.

All of the girls are rated from 0 to 3, based on their poise, speaking ability, carriage, and attractiveness. "0" connotes a girl who has no chance to win; "1" might be called back; a "2" could be a Rose princess. A "3" is a potential queen. From the twenty-five finalists, seven princesses are chosen, and one week later the queen is chosen from among the princesses.

The Queen of the Roses is not just queen for a day; she reigns a bit each day from October to January, appearing at approximately one hundred events prior to the Tournament of Roses parade. Then, on the day of the parade (New Year's Day), the queen rides on the central float among sixty-one flower-studded floats. She sits on her throne and waves to the throng as she travels the five-and-a-half-mile parade route from Orange Grove Boulevard down Colorado Avenue in the center of Pasadena. Later the queen is an honored guest at the Rose Bowl game, where her regal presence adds a note of courtly pageantry to the scrimmages of modern-day gladiators.

ACADEMIC

Receive an Honorary Doctorate ─────────────

Right now you are probably thinking: "I couldn't win an honorary degree. I barely graduated from college." The cap and gown and brightly colored hood can still be within your grasp if you've attained prominence by doing what you do well, even if you are not academically inclined. The cachet of an honorary doctorate is that it puts a stamp of approval on your work. You become someone to be reckoned with. Colleges enjoy having a mix of scholars and "real world" types to bring a special panache to commencement exercises.

The selection process will vary from college to college, but Columbia's procedure seems to be typical. Nominations are solicited from the university faculty. A special university Senate committee on honors and prizes looks over the list and also nominates on its own. This committee then breaks into four subcommittees in different fields. They review the names and narrow the list to twenty-five. Then they meet with the executive committee of trustees and select the top ten (the trustees vote). The president writes to the candidates and asks if they can come to the ceremony. Generally speaking, degrees are awarded only to those who can come to the university. By appearing at commencement you are, in a way, swapping prestige with the university.

Some colleges look for popular writers for favorable publicity and have rewarded Art Buchwald, Alex Haley, William Peter Blatty, Isaac Asimov, and Kurt Vonnegut, Jr., with hoods. Other colleges scout around for show business types and confer academic stature on such performers as Nina Simone, Frank Sinatra, Perry Como, Richard Widmark, and Joanne Woodward. The Tonight Show could conceivably line up an all-academic guest list that might include Dr. Julia Child, Dr. Julie Harris, Dr. Gary Trudeau, and Dr. Danny Kaye.

Check into your own alma mater's honorary degrees, and keep the alumni office abreast of your activities. Keep donating money to the alumni fund—like some Arabian potentates who shall remain nameless—and don't be surprised if you receive a letter from a college president asking what size you take in a cap and gown.

Earn a Phi Beta Kappa Key ⸻

Phi Beta Kappa keys are not for the key chain, they are to be worn, to be noticed, to mingle with other gold keys worn by other Phi Betes. Phi Beta Kappa is the most important honor society in academia today, and its key symbolizes admittance to the society, a reward for undergraduate excellence in scholarship in the liberal arts and sciences. Phi Beta Kappa is elitist in the best sense of the word: it attempts to maintain high academic standards of scholarship despite the onslaught of new "pop culture" courses, widespread illiteracy in college, and the lowering of academic standards in many parts of the nation. As standards decline, the society holds aloft a banner proclaiming—from the Greek words whose initials form its name—"love of wisdom is the guide to life."

When you receive your Phi Beta Kappa key, you'll be in the company of more than 380,000 people who have been elected to the society during the past two hundred years; most of whom are still around to twiddle their keys. If you do manage to get into the society, you'll be in the company of thirteen of our Presidents, including John Quincy Adams, Woodrow Wilson, Theodore and Franklin Roosevelt. Six of the nine current Supreme Court justices have keys (presumably somewhere under their black robes).

The way to get in is to get top grades in college, because the society will choose from among the top 10 per cent of the nation's graduating class. There is often difficulty in evaluating certain types of new courses—skeet shooting, Icelandic studies, advanced sex education—but if you've been getting straight As with a smattering of Bs and if you go to a college that has a chapter of the society (there are 214 university and college chapters, 46 regional associations), you should be able to get a key.

Symbolically, the Phi Beta Kappa key is a key to knowledge, but don't be surprised if it opens up a lot of other doors as well.

Earn Admission to the Harvard Business School

The Harvard University Graduate School of Business is the most prestigious business school in the Western Hemisphere. The "B" School has turned out more presidents and board chairmen of major corporations, more key executives and decision makers, than any other business school in the country. It is the oldest, largest, and most celebrated business school in the United States. More importantly, it's located only a few miles from Joyce Chen's Restaurant, the best Chinese restaurant north of New York's Chinatown.

Of the 750 to 800 men and women who are admitted to the two-year program in business administration, the average age is 25.8 and 80 per cent have had an average of three years of full-time business experience or military duty. Each of the newly admitted students has demonstrated either an ability of a managerial nature or a special intellectual gift.

If you're thinking of applying, you'll be happy to know that the school requires no degree for admission. In fact, Harvard Business School is likely to take major risks in admitting students whose qualitative test scores are below the 96th percentile. The "B" School doesn't have to prove itself: it has made its reputation and can afford to look not just at grades but at proven eminence in the form of excellent work experience and personal leadership ability.

When you apply, you'll be faced with the Business School's

classy 17-page application form. The form is divided into three categories: (1) academic (grade-point average, mathematical and verbal aptitude test results, and admission scores); (2) work experience (judged on responses to the questions posed and detailed recommendation of employers); (3) personal considerations (applicants' statements give insights into the reasons for applying, level of maturity, career goals, and what the applicants expect to gain from and contribute to the program).

Your application will be evaluated by several of the half dozen full-time administrators hired to sort out the incoming class. The applications are screened by the administrators, who send their choices to the dean; the dean further reduces the pile of applications until about 700 students have been chosen from the 3,500 or so applicants.

Harvard places some emphasis on insuring a demographic and socioeconomic balance in their classes. Therefore it is quite possible that you could matriculate at Harvard Business School without having been valedictorian at your undergraduate school.

So if happiness is a three-piece suit, a subscription to *Forbes,* and a corner office, point yourself to that lovely cluster of Georgian buildings on the Charles River known as the Harvard Business School. If you think of yourself as a self-made man or woman and Harvard turns you off, you can always mind your own business or apply to Wharton.

Gain Admission to West Point (*The United States Military Academy*) _____

To say that you are a cadet implies not only brains but the discipline and physical stamina that set you apart from other undergraduates and shape you in the mold of West Point alumni like Lee, Grant, MacArthur, and Eisenhower. West Point wants each candidate to be seventeen to twenty-two years of age by July 1 of the year admitted, a U.S. citizen at time of enrollment (exception: foreign students nominated by agreement between the United States and another country), unmarried, trustworthy, emotionally stable, and motivated.

Academically speaking, each student should have an above-average high school or college academic record, strong performance on the American College Testing (ACT) Assessment Program exam or the College Board Admissions Testing Program Scholastic Aptitude Test (SAT), and recommendations from the principal, counselors, teachers, or other officials who can judge the applicant's character and academic potential.

Most colleges don't care if you're a physical wreck as long as your brain is in working order. West Point finds out what shape you're in by combining your performance on the Physical Aptitude Examination (PAE) and an evaluation of your athletic record. The PAE consists of four events: pull-ups for men (palms away from face; or flexed-arm hang for women (for time); basketball throw (from kneeling position); standing long jump, and 300-yard shuttle run. Your PAE score is a combination of your best efforts on each of the four events. A high or low score on any one test item does not determine success or failure on the entire PAE.

Although medical evaluation standards differ among the various commissioning programs of the armed services, only one medical examination is needed to meet the application requirements of all service academies and the four-year ROTC scholarship program. Among the items with which West Point is concerned are visual acuity, muscle balance, color vision, refraction error, and standards of height. Men must stand a minimum of 60 inches tall and a maximum of 80 inches; women may range in height anywhere from 58 to 72 inches.

West Point will start a candidate file for you upon receipt of your completed Pre-Candidate Questionnaire. But before the Military Academy can consider you for admission you must be nominated for a commission by an authorized official. Commissions are allocated by law to the Vice-President; members of Congress; congressional delegates from Washington, D.C., the Virgin Islands, and Guam; governors of Puerto Rico, the Canal Zone, and American Samoa; and to the Department of the

Army. A nominating official may select up to ten young men and women to compete for each cadetship vacancy he may have. Apply for a nomination from each source for which you qualify.

After going through the West Point admissions process, fighting in a war should be child's play.

Win a Rhodes Scholarship

There are scholarships and scholarships, but a Rhodes scholarship is something to write home about. And if you win one you *will* be writing home, because the scholarship entitles you to two fully supported years at Oxford University in England.

If you are between the ages of eighteen and twenty-four, unmarried, have a distinguished record of intellectual achievement and a range of extracurricular activities, you may be among the next group of Rhodes scholarship winners. You must have your bachelor's degree by the time you start at Oxford, and you'll be happy to know that you may get married after one year's residence at Oxford.

The first thing to do is to get the attention of the state committee on the Rhodes scholarships in your home state or the state in which you attend college. The secretary of each state committee (there is a committee in each of the fifty states) receives your application and gathers a dossier on you, complete with college transcripts, letters of recommendation, and comments by committee interviewers. The people who interview you are not only interested in your academic qualifications and the broad scope of your outside interests, but they also look for people "not indifferent to exercise." In other words, you don't have to be a Junior Phi Bete and an All American . . . but it helps. Onetime Rhodes scholars include Dean Rusk, Justice Byron "Whizzer" White, Bill Bradley, Charles Collingwood, and Kris Kristofferson.

Each state committee recommends two finalists for consideration in district competitions. There are eight districts in the United States, and each district designates four Rhodes scholars.

These gifted individuals are treated to two years at Oxford, with the possibility of a one-year extension in certain cases. They study in every imaginable field, including medicine, poetry, law, classics, physics, and anthropology. Sleeping in buildings built three centuries ago, these young men and women can look forward to writing papers for tutors, strolling in peaceful quadrangles, and adjusting to English cooking.

BUSINESS/MONEY

Obtain a $100,000 Bank Loan

Remember the old adage, "It takes money to make money"? The fellow who said it was probably a banker.

Picture this: you're sitting in your bank making small talk with a loan officer. Great rapport. You look terrific: Upmann cigar, Bill Blass tie, Yves St. Laurent suit, Gucci loafers. Then you spring it—you'd like to borrow $100,000. It seems that a 24-foot cabin cruiser is on "special" this week. Suddenly a chill comes over the conversation and your friendly banker begins treating you as if your Ban Roll-On had just rolled off.

Loan officers are accustomed to making loans for new Datsuns, new sun porches, and root-canal work, but asking for a hundred grand for your personal use is more than likely to be a conversation-stopper. Savings banks won't advance you a nickel more than you have in your bank account, and even commercial banks consider loans of that size "small business loans," as if there were something obscene in needing that kind of money for pure fun.

Before the vault door swings open, a loan officer will certainly broach a sticky subject: collateral. They don't wish to seem impolite, but they'd prefer not being swindled, if it can be avoided. Even if you've been banking at the same branch for twenty years and play golf with its president, you still have to prove to the bank that, in case of disaster, you won't attempt to flee to Morocco. If you have $100,000 invested in stocks or bonds, you'll have no problem getting a secured loan, but if all you have is a Pepsodent smile, great expectations, and a shoestring, don't expect a miracle.

Let's say that you approach a commercial bank for $100,000 loan to start a new business. Their first question is likely to be: "Have you ever been in business before?" If you have been a successful businessman, you must try to prove to the banker that lightning will certainly strike twice in the same place. If you have not been successful, delete any reference to the above homily. Beware: a bank may have the audacity to ask you for a financial statement showing assets, liabilities, and net worth. If you are not even worth the price of a net, don't bluff. If your financial *statement* is more like a *question,* save it to show to your tax auditor. With money as tight as a banker's smile, your chances of getting a start-up loan are practically nil—unless you have assets in sufficient quantity and quality to satisfy the bank's requirements. Otherwise, they'll probably ask you to start with a smaller figure.

It may take about a year for you to establish yourself as a candidate for an unsecured $100,000 loan. First, borrow $10,000, secure it, and pay it back in ninety days. Then borrow $30,000 (partially secured) and pay it back in sixty days. Then borrow $60,000 (only partially secured) and repay it promptly. Now you've become a good bet, and a bank may well agree to lend you $100,000 with only a minimum of collateral.

Some factors that can help your chances: a good personal credit card record, a respectable Dun and Bradstreet rating, and a reliable financial track record. A Christmas card to your loan officer wouldn't hurt either.

If you're successful, you'll probably get your $100,000 with the interest already deducted, unless you wish to pay the interest at a later date.

Try another bank if the first one turns you down. When the second bank rebuffs you, point yourself toward the Small Business Administration (armed with two letters of rejection) and apply for money through the SBA's bank-guaranteed loan program. If you qualify, you might be able to borrow directly from SBA at low interest. However, these loans are for soberer enterprises than impressing the neighborhood yacht club. Ask yourself if you really want that cabin cruiser—especially with the price of gas what it is today. I mean, be *sensible.* . . .

Sit on the Board of a
Fortune *Magazine Top Ten Corporation* _____

How glorious it must be to sit on the board of a giant corporation especially when you've come in from outside the company and are uninvolved in internal politics. High-powered executives are commonly invited to sit on the boards of companies that bear no relationship to their home firms. These men and women are not cardboard stereotypes from the cartoons of *The New Yorker* but corporate watchdogs whose outside expertise and advice to management keep the company honest and earn them high respect. At Texaco, General Motors, Exxon, and other corporations listed among *Fortune's* top ten, non-company directors outnumber company-affiliated directors. As one examines the backgrounds of these "visiting" directors, an image emerges.

Born in 1921 to upper-middle-class parents, he attended private school before matriculating at Harvard at the tail end of the Depression. When the war came he was commissioned as a second lieutenant and saw action in the Pacific. Upon leaving the service, he resumed his education at night and accepted a sales position at a small pharmaceutical company. When he married the girl he took to the Junior Prom, he was earning less than $4,500 a year. After being with the company for three years he was able to begin a Master's program in economics. He graduated with honors and was promoted to general manager. In 1963 the pharmaceutical company was bought by a conglomerate, and in 1965 he became a vice-president of the conglomerate. In 1970 he became a director. He now lives in the suburbs of Connecticut, belongs to the Links, has a summer home in Boothbay Harbor, Maine, and a small Park Avenue *pied-à-terre*.

His wife is chairperson of two charity groups, one political party, and a woman's group, and his son is engaged to a lovely blonde from Katonah whose sister was once Julie Nixon Eisenhower's college roommate. Our director has received three honorary degrees from junior colleges, has played golf with the secretary of HEW, and sits on the boards of three other companies, one of which has appeared regularly on *Fortune*'s Top Ten list. He attends theatre every few weeks, smokes an occasional cigar, and has been known to awaken at five-thirty to jog with his Labrador retriever, Captain. He works from 10 A.M. to 6:15 P.M. and does his board work as his schedule allows. He plans to retire early, sell his homes, buy a thirty-foot yawl, sail to Aruba, and spend his remaining days studying ecology.

His replacement? Born in 1944 in a suburban Connecticut village . . .

Insure Your Property with Lloyd's of London ────────────────

While some insurance companies liken themselves to cities, rocks, and volcanoes, and spend thousands of dollars slapping their own backs on numerous television commercials, Lloyd's of London marches on, the strong silent type. Lloyd's is not actually an insurance company but rather a group of underwriters who approve loans for various Lloyd's syndicates. There are more than three hundred Lloyd's syndicates, and their members pledge their personal fortunes, as well as the fortunes of their heirs, that your insurance will be paid off in full if you have a legitimate claim.

Lloyd's of London paid off more than $100,000,000 on the damage caused by the San Francisco earthquake, while many other insurers went broke trying to honor their commitments. They also paid mightily for losses incurred on the *Andrea Doria* and the *Titanic* disasters. But perhaps Lloyd's is best known for their unique policies designed for events and people of international importance. They've insured Durante's nose, Callas' voice, Dietrich's legs, and Nikita Khrushchev's safety during his 1959 trip to the United States, as well as the on-time opening of the 1964 New York World's Fair. While Lloyd's prefers to insure property rather than clients' lives, they did manage to create a

special policy for the astronauts that included coverage for "air travel."

To insure your race horse or a piece of jewelry, you probably would not be able to go directly to a Lloyd's underwriter until a licensed insurer in the United States had attempted to find a company willing to write the policy. Should several insurance companies refuse to write a policy for you, the broker could then legally go to an excess line insurer such as Lloyd's ("excess line" means insurance that normally cannot be placed with regular insurance brokers). However, in Illinois and Kentucky, Lloyd's is licensed and in those states a person needing insurance could deal directly with Lloyd's for his individual insurance needs.

Don't be put off if Lloyd's keeps a low profile. Their underwriters and the limited number of brokers who are permitted to place risks at Lloyd's are restricted in their rights to advertise. They live by a discreet code and never discuss a client's losses or risks undertaken. It's not reticence but modesty.

Acquire a Seat on the New York Stock Exchange _____

For the dubious distinction of trading stocks and earning a commission instead of paying one, the New York Stock Exchange puts one through an elaborate rite of passage.

There is a thick paperback book titled *Constitution and Rules* which the New York Stock Exchange publishes. It contains the myriad rules and regulations describing every conceivable way to become a member, to finance your membership, and how, under certain circumstances, the membership may be taken away from you. This book does not make good beach reading.

You must be of "the minimum age of majority required to be responsible for your contracts" in each jurisdiction in which you conduct your business, a citizen of the United States, and able to pass a physical examination given by the Stock Exchange. Assuming you're healthy, submit three letters of reference and be sponsored by two members or allied members of the Exchange of at least one year's standing (your references and sponsors cannot be merely casual social or business acquaintances). It also helps if you have passing acquaintance with such Street-wise expressions as "tight money," "technical rally," and "short-term interest."

You can pay for your seat on the Exchange from your own funds, receive it as a gift, obtain a loan from a member organization of the Exchange, obtain a subordinated loan.

According to legend, the Stock Exchange was founded under a buttonwood tree in 1797 when the twenty-four original members agreed to meet regularly with each other to buy and sell shares in the business ventures of the day.

Things have gotten a bit more complex since then. There are now 1,366 members of the Exchange (that is the maximum number of seats on the Exchange). The price of each seat has fluctuated from about $700,000 (before the crash of '29) to about $17,000 (early in World War II). If you are bullish on America and your health is good, and there is a seat available, the price of a seat at this writing is about $50,000. You will also be obligated to pay 10 per cent of the purchase price to the Exchange as a fee, and you'll be required to contribute 1 per cent of your net annual commissions to the Exchange. The rest is easy: just follow Bernard Baruch's advice to "buy low and sell high."

Open a Credit Account with New York's Palace Restaurant (and Dine Sheik to Sheik) ___

What's the most money you've ever plunked down for dinner? Fifty dollars? A hundred? A hundred and fifty? At New York's Palace Restaurant the average check for two, including tax and tip, is about $225. Gratuities for waiters, captain, maître d'hôtel, and sommelier are included in your bill and they amount to ap-

proximately 24 per cent of the check. Overpriced, you say? Craig Claiborne, one of America's most knowledgeable gourmets, says that eating at the Palace "is the finest experience I've had outside France." Gael Greene, restaurant critic of *New York* magazine, regards her dinner at the Palace as one of the great sensual delights of her life.

Eating at the Palace is like eating in a fine home (a fine home that also happens to be a temple of sybaritic epicureanism). The décor is tasteful, not pretentious, and the eight-course meal is served leisurely but efficiently over a period of several hours. The Palace accommodates fifty people—fifty rich people—who dine from china plates that cost as much as thirty dollars each, and from the finest crystal stemware. The clientele walk on pastel flowered carpeting, sit on love seats and silk-upholstered armchairs, and bask in the glow of candlelight reflected from silver candlesticks. Still think it's overpriced?

You won't think so when Chef Michel Fitoussi (formerly of Lutèce) creates his oysters flecked with caviar, or a magnificent rack of lamb. Perhaps a bottle of Château Lafite Rothschild '52 to complement your dinner? Are you weakening?

You're welcome to pay cash, or put your feast on Visa, American Express, Diners Club, or Master Charge, but you might want to open a house account with owner Frank Valenza. He'll be happy to give you a gold—that's *solid* gold—credit card, provided you are in the habit of giving his restaurant approximately $10,000 worth of business a year. If you're just interested in popping in for an ocasional beef Wellington, you won't qualify for one. After all, it costs the owner about $600 to have each one made.

Establish a Credit Line in Las Vegas ──────────

Why is it that, every day, people whom God never meant to play
games of chance riskier than Old Maid walk into casinos and in-
stantly wager everything except the gold in their teeth on the
wild ricochets of a steel ball on a whirling roulette wheel?

If you lose your last chip the house will probably be happy to
extend credit. All they have to do is get on the phone to an outfit
known as Central Credit and find out everything they always
wanted to know about how you pay your bills. Central Credit is
a clearinghouse for such credit matters, and they're the ones who
make sure that your good or bad reputation follows you wher-
e'er you go. Whether or not you use your credit, it marks you as
a man of the world, a person who is comfortable in an atmos-
phere that intimidates those who have set themselves a ten-dollar
limit for the evening.

Generally speaking, you apply for a credit line at a Las Vegas
or a Caribbean casino by filling out an application (name, address, name of business, position, name of bank—the usual
stuff); Central Credit will help the casino ascertain your bank's
opinion of you and some details about your checking account's
usual balance. They do not make recommendations about individuals; they simply furnish information.

At the MGM Grand Hotel, management prefers that you do
not extend the credit requested at the start of any one evening of
gambling. If you want more credit tomorrow, fine, but they prefer you to "sleep on it," and not act rashly. After all, casinos do
not want to earn the reputation of cleaning people out—it's bad
for business. Rumor has it that Frank Sinatra once exceeded his
$200,000 credit line at the Sands and was angry when further
credit was denied him. Part of the reason he was annoyed was
that he was co-owner of the hotel at the time.

Hotels are loath to discuss the highest credit lines ever given by
their casinos, but rumor has it that it exceeds several million dollars. Table stakes vary and are often decided by a group of gam-

blers themselves, rather than by the casino. So, in that 120-yard-long casino at the MGM Grand, there have been some wildly expensive games of chance. Things are getting bigger all the time: there's a casino under construction in Reno that will be even larger than the one at the Grand Hotel.

If you're a two-bit gambler, go to the Golden Nugget in downtown Las Vegas. You probably won't need credit there, because you can play for dimes and quarters, and drinks are on the house.

Obtain a 5A1 Dun and Bradstreet Rating for your Company _____

Located in twenty-six countries and across America, Dun and Bradstreet is the business community's criterion for determining and making known a particular company's economic strength or lack thereof. A healthy "D & B" tells the world that your company has a solid financial track record, pays its bills promptly and can be trusted. The highest rating obtainable is 5A1. The 5A refers to an estimated financial status in excess of $50,000,000. The 1 denotes excellence in matters such as bank balances, customers, financial statements, company background and personnel. The most important criterion for determining the rating your company earns is its bank and financial statements and the opinion of its creditors on matters like the prompt payment of bills.

Generally, you'll get a D & B rating after a company has inquired about you, and after Dun and Bradstreet has answered that inquiry with a report. Sometimes a new company will call Dun and Bradstreet to offer information about their new enterprise, but most of the time Dun and Bradstreet responds to an inquiry from one of its subscribers. Dun and Bradstreet will usually interview the principal of a company before issuing its report; the appraisal by an expert analyst is the basis of your rating. A reference book containing the latest gradings of each company is published every two months. A check is made on graded companies once a year, and an interim revision is made every six months.

You don't need $50,000,000 in your back pocket to be of interest to Dun and Bradstreet. If your capital is between $5,000 and $9,000 your company will be rated GG, but even a GG is fine if you also have a 1 attached to it. The all-important 1 (or even 2, which is good) tells a credit manager to approve your order without much hesitation; it tells him that you're good for the money.

Be an "Angel" for a Broadway Show ───────────

If you want security in your investments, go to Merrill Lynch, but you can add a touch of glamor to your portfolio and participate in the creation of a new work of art by investing in a Broadway show.

Shubert Alley is replete with tall tales involving overnight riches, one-day wipe-outs, and valiant artistic successes struggling to find enough of an audience to remain alive. Producers woo investors' dollars in order to launch every new play and musical.

Even successful producers like Harold Prince still need to capture new investors to help finance such productions as *Company,* *A Little Night Music,* and *Follies.* David Merrick, perhaps the producer with the best track record on Broadway, has maintained the same loyal investors over his long career.

Typically, a producer will send a letter to known "angels" describing the proposed production, telling them why he feels it stands a good chance of succeeding (a major star, good reviews elsewhere, etc.), and a projection of what the capitalization will be. The letter is not a formal solicitation of funds. The solicitation is made when the S.E.C. (Securities and Exchange Commission) draws up papers and a prospectus is sent out to potential investors. In his letter to investors in *Side by Side by*

Sondheim, Prince wrote: "I'm always asked whether I'm enthusiastic about a project by potential investors, and I'm always tempted to reply that I wouldn't be doing it if I weren't. Well, I am and I would."

Producer Morton Gottlieb was once asked, "Who makes up the investors?" He replied: "Anyone you can get ahold of," but it's rare that a producer locates a first-time backer such as the woman who, without even reading the script, wrote out a check for $42,000 (for Gottlieb's *Same Time, Next Year*).

If you want to invest, start reading the trade magazines (e.g., *Variety, Backstage,* and *Show Business*) and studying the reports about upcoming productions. Musicals and comedies are usually better bets than straight plays. A major star (e.g., Liv Ullmann) or top writer (e.g., Neil Simon) will help secure at least modest success for some shows, but many are pure speculation. Write the producer and ask to be kept in mind as a possible investor. Unless he already has backers, he'll surely keep you very much in mind, if not for the current production, then for future productions. The good plays have not always been gobbled up by insiders and film companies months in advance. Just remember that Cole Porter's *Kiss Me Kate* needed more than a hundred backers' auditions before it was fully capitalized.

Attend a few backers' auditions—those bare-bones runthroughs wherein producers pry checks from potential investors —and never forget that along Shubert Alley a "sure thing" can always go the way of *Kean, Mata Hari,* or *1600 Pennsylvania Avenue.*

Find a Top Literary Agent to Sell Your Book

As someone once remarked, "Everyone is a contestant in the immortality sweepstakes." One way of achieving a kind of immortality is to have your book published. The best way to go about it is to get a literary agent to represent you. If you happen to be Henry Kissinger or Liv Ullmann, an agent may approach you, but for most would-be authors it's vice versa.

Most agents pick up new clients among the friends and acquaintances of their present clients. Your best bet is to ask a friend who's had something published if he'll read your writing. If you don't know any published writers, you could turn to magazines like *The Writer* or *Writer's Digest* to gain hints about finding an agent, but watch out for agents who advertise their services. (Good agents do not advertise.) Another obvious starting place is the Yellow Pages. New York's Yellow Pages contain the names of more than a hundred literary agents. Keep mental notes on the ones you've heard about (e.g., "So-and-so is the best," "So-and-so has no clout," "So-and-so has just started in the business"). Pick a few, write to them, and tell them what you've got. Meanwhile, take a trip to the library and check out these sources:[1]

Publishers Weekly

PW is publishing's leading trade magazine and it often contains information about new literary agents, as well as information about agents who have just closed important deals. Don't approach an agent simply because he seems to have a lot of squibs in *PW* (some agents are selling themselves rather than books), although, obviously, an agent with big-name authors will probably have access to a wider variety of contacts (i.e., have clout).

Literary Market Place

Known as *LMP,* this annual compendium contains a comprehensive list of America's most active agents and agencies. It provides addresses, telephone numbers, and the type of material in which each agent specializes (fiction, non-fiction, plays, etc.).

---

[1] *Publishers Weekly* and *Literary Market Place* are published by the R. R. Bowker Company, 1180 Avenue of the Americas, New York, N.Y. 10036.

With editors often playing musical chairs, job-hopping all over the publishing world, and with huge conglomerates absorbing the once small, gentlemanly business of publishing, more emphasis is being placed on finding an agent who is a known quantity. Don't be fooled into thinking that the most highly visible agents are the best. Agents are notorious for publicizing puffed-up figures on the deals they've recently negotiated, and the big agents are often too swamped to pay much attention to a new author unless he's already been published. Look for an agent who specializes in selling the type of book you've written, one who is willing to help you develop as a writer. Ideally, a good agent combines the best features of P. T. Barnum, Alfred Knopf, Louis Nizer, and St. Francis of Assisi.

By all means, contact the Society of Authors' Representatives and ask for a copy of their leaflet titled "The Literary Agent." The leaflet will not only fill you in on what an agent can and cannot do for you but will also tell you about agents' standard practices and how to submit your work to an agent. Remember: there are no credentials necessary to be a literary agent. Hence, if you doubt an agent's methods, you can always check with S.A.R. for sound advice.

Not every good agent is a member of the society (which is only for New York-based agents who have been in business a minimum of three years). Scott Meredith, who handles Norman Mailer and Spiro Agnew, among others, is not a member. However, Sterling Lord, whose clients include Erica Jong and Jimmy Breslin, belongs to the society. Remember that even some of the top literary agencies can't make an unsalable book suddenly salable.[2]

If your book has potential, somewhere there is an agent ready to sign you up. Just remember: never mail out your only copy of what you've written, and don't sign any agreement without first reading it carefully. Very carefully.

[2] If you're curious about how to present your manuscript to a publisher, consult *Writer's Market '78*, edited by Jane Koester and Bruce Joel Hillman (*Writer's Digest*), 894 pp., $13.95.

SPORTS

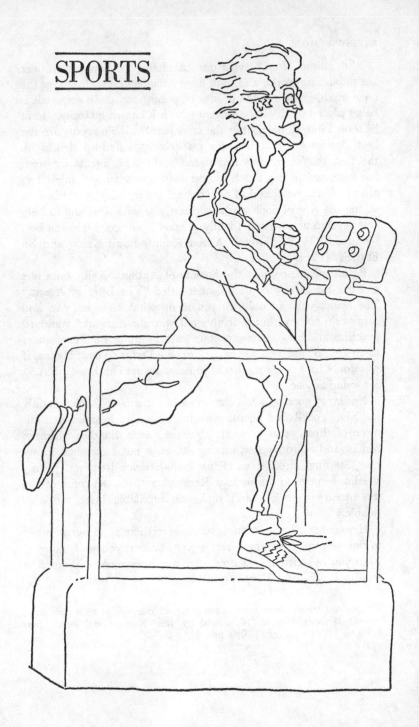

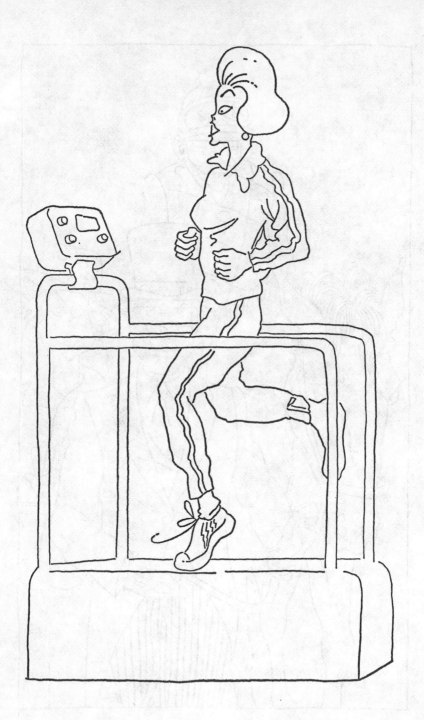

Register Your Horse and Silks
with the Jockey Club

Mickey and Karen Taylor went to a yearling auction, and Mickey bought Karen a $17,500 yearling. As a lark, they entered their horse in a race and he won. He kept on winning and winning and eventually he won the Triple Crown of racing: the Kentucky Derby, the Preakness, and the Belmont Stakes. The horse's name is Seattle Slew, and, like every thoroughbred racer, he was registered with the Jockey Club.

The Jockey Club has nothing to do with riders, only with the animals they ride. Breeders and owners register their horses for the purpose of clearly identifying the animals and to maintain the thoroughbred studbook. The registration application, a very precise form, requires the name of the foal's owner, breeder, present owner of the mare, where the foal was born (the Jockey Club registers horses dropped in Cuba and Canada as well as in the United States) and the horse's identifiable color and markings. A service (breeding) certificate, which gives further details of the youngster's pedigree, must be included with the application.

The certificate and application information is fed into a computer, and before long you are the proud registrant of a thoroughbred. (By the way, the service certificate folderol, which sometimes wrings one's withers, makes it easier for you to document and register succeeding foals.)

The Jockey Club dictates that a horse's name contain a prescribed maximum number of letters and spaces. Your horse cannot be named after, or be a variation on the name of, a great past thoroughbred (e.g., there will never be another Man o' War) or be named anything obscene or suggestive.

If you think that registering a horse is a complex procedure, just wait until you have to choose the silks that the horse's jockey will wear. You can tell a horse's owner by identifying the unique combination of color and design worn by the horse's jockey. If a jockey were to ride for three different owners in the same day he would change silks each time. The Jockey Club's application form for registration of silks offers a variety of design and color combinations. You choose the design and colors you wish, and a Jockey Club official tries to reconcile your wishes with patterns as yet untaken.

A rule of thumb is that the more understated the pattern the more prestigious and well established the owner. The Phipps family's silks—black with a red cap—are simple, classic, and elegant, but you may go in for things like sashes, stripes, or chevrons (or you may have to, because all the basics have been taken). Some people base their designs on personal interests: composer Burt Bacharach has two "B" notes. Since more than 14,000 thoroughbreds have been registered with the Jockey Club (with about 800 to 1,000 new ones added each year), you may not be able to get primary colors for your own potential Derby winner, but keep in mind that silks don't make the horse.

Qualify to Compete in the Masters Golf Tournament _____

Augusta, Georgia, is to golfers what Louisville, Kentucky, is to thoroughbreds: a place to prove yourself before a mass audience, stiff competition, and the legendary reputations of former greats. Probably everyone who has ever putted around the house has wondered just how one rates the opportunity to do his putting in Augusta.

If you are a previous Masters champion, you have a lifetime invitation to compete, and if you're a U. S. Open winner, your invitation is good for five years. An American or British amateur champion will be invited for two years following his title win, and practically all other invitees (Ryder Cup team members, Walker Cup members, P.G.A. champs, etc.) are welcome to compete in a prescribed number of Masters following their particular championships or awards. In addition, the Masters is open to the first twenty-four players in the past year's Masters, first sixteen players in the U. S. Open, and first eight players in the previous P.G.A. championship.

The usual field in the Masters is seventy-five or eighty, a mixture of professionals and amateurs, Americans and foreigners. Filling out this prestigious field is the British Open champion and semi-finalists in the previous year's U. S. Amateur Championships. Winners of any major P.G.A. co-sponsored tour tournament may gain eligibility from the finish of one Masters tournament to the start of the next.

No winter rules at Augusta, no Mulligan, no do-overs. Golfers come here to compete for $40,000 first prize and the sartorial status of donning the traditional green jacket. They can expect some stiff competition from Mr. Nicklaus, who has donned five green jackets, and they can expect to be watched by a home audience of more than 25,000,000.

As you know, an invitation to the Masters is not for those who are duffers. You can always go to Augusta as a spectator. You may not win any prizes, but you'll enjoy learning what makes a professional golfer so good. Like the rich, professional golfers *are* different.

Try Out for the Cincinnati Redlegs _____

Trying out for a baseball team requires more than just a mitt, some guts, and a fondness for chewing tobacco. Most of the Sunday hot shots who fight for a quick look-see during spring training usually wilt when they hear the sizzle of a 100-m.p.h. fast ball. However, if you want a chance to show your talents, the best thing to do is to catch the eye of a big league scout.

With players like Bench, Rose, and Foster, the Cincinnati Redlegs are *the* team of the seventies. Cincinnati has scouts all across the United States, and a phone call to Riverfront Stadium will give you the name of the scout in your area. Protocol dictates that you write a letter to the scout care of the Redlegs (write "Attention: Scouting" on the envelope) and tell the scout a bit about your background. See if you can arrange to have the scout catch you in action—at your high school, college, league, or sand lot—and see if you can meet him later and, over a quick glass of Gatorade, discuss your potential to play major league baseball. If you haven't been scouted by age twenty, better hang up your spikes.

A good scout will go out of his way to see a promising ballplayer, and you have nothing to lose by trying your luck. The scout looks for the telltale signs of the incipient professional as well as for the obvious attribute of power at the plate. Can you hit both right-handers and southpaws? If you're an infielder, can you make the long throw from deep in the hole at shortstop? How good are you at shaving with a Trac II razor?

If you make a favorable impression on the scout he may ask you to come to spring training or sign you to a minor league contract. Depending on your talent and experience, you'll play either A, AA, or AAA ball, with Triple A ball being the closest to major league competition.

If you do get to spring training, you'll be one of forty men trying to gain one of twenty-five positions on the squad. Every thought is directed toward being in the dugout, in the bullpen, or (preferably) on the field when the umpire yells, "Play ball!" on opening day in Cincinnati. As a major leaguer, you'll be paid minimum salary of $20,000 prorated over the entire year. Not bad for a rookie, eh?

Gain a Place in the Baseball Hall of Fame _____

There are several ways to get into the Baseball Hall of Fame: one is to drive up to Cooperstown, New York, and walk in, but the correct way is to be voted in because of your accomplishments as a player.

Assuming you've been an active major league ballplayer some-
time within the past twenty years and have been retired for a
minimum of five years, you're eligible. You must have played at
least ten years (or in ten different seasons), and, needless to say,
you should have hit more than a few Texas leaguers in an occasional All-Star Game. About 400 members of the Baseball
Writers' Association cast votes. Sports editors are eligible to vote,
even though they're not in the press box, and even copymen who
have been handling baseball copy for ten years have a chance to
vote (in San Francisco, where the Giants have played for more
than a decade, the writers, editors, and copymen have just
recently become eligible to vote for Hall of Famers).

Eligible members of the Baseball Writers' Association vote for
up to ten eligible people (most vote for only four or five) once a
year, usually in January. There is no count as to how each writer
ranks the players he lists, but if a man is listed on 75 per cent of
the ballots, he's in the Hall of Fame.

If you miss out on election to the Hall of Fame (as Phil Riz-
zuto did—his last playing year was 1956, and he did not receive
the required votes for admission), there is still an opportunity to
be voted in as a Baseball Veteran. A separate committee of
twelve regularly meets in person (usually in the winter) to consider eligible candidates:

Players who have been retired from the major leagues as
players for at least twenty-five years prior to the election and
who are no longer eligible in the elections held by the Baseball
Writers' Association of America. They must have competed in at
least ten championship seasons in the major leagues as baseball
players.

Baseball executives and/or managers and/or umpires who
have been retired from organized baseball (as executives, managers, or umpires) for at least five years prior to election. The
five-year waiting period may be reduced to six months for anyone who has reached the age of sixty-five.

The committee is authorized to elect no more than two
members to the National Baseball Hall of Fame each year from
those eligible as players, and only one from those eligible as executives, managers, or umpires.

There are no automatic elections based on performance, such as a batting average of .400 or pitching a perfect game. If you don't make it, you can comfort yourself with the knowledge that if .400 hitters and perfect-game pitchers don't always measure up, what are you worried about?

Race in the Indianapolis "500"

Being a Paul Newman fan and having a heavy foot on the accelerator aren't enough.

You need a sponsor, someone willing to invest the necessary capital to build a four-wheeled vehicle capable of speeds in excess of 200 miles per hour. The car must be registered in the United States Auto Club and comply with U.S.A.C. rules (in terms of size, engine, etc.). The owner is the entrant; it is he who selects a driver and crew. Drivers should possess knowledge, experience, and quick reflexes. They should know the difference between a V-12 Volker Olmstead and a turbocharged AMC stockblock unit as well as most people know their own names. It's no wonder that, in 1977, only eleven of the thirty-three drivers were under forty years of age.

Each year eighty or ninety cars come to compete in the qualifying heats that will decide the occupants of the thirty-three positions on the field when the race is run. The track opens for practice and qualifying heats about three weeks before the day of the race (the last Sunday in May). Each one of the four qualifying days has its own special interest to racing fans. The pole position ("pole sitter") is decided the first day, going to the day's fastest qualifier. The pole position is the dream of every driver whose sponsor has paid the $1,000 entry fee that accompanies the entry form. Drivers are allowed up to three warm-up laps, then must take the green flag for the qualifying attempt or get off the track. If the driver fails to signal an official start, he is not charged with the attempt but he must go to the end of the line.

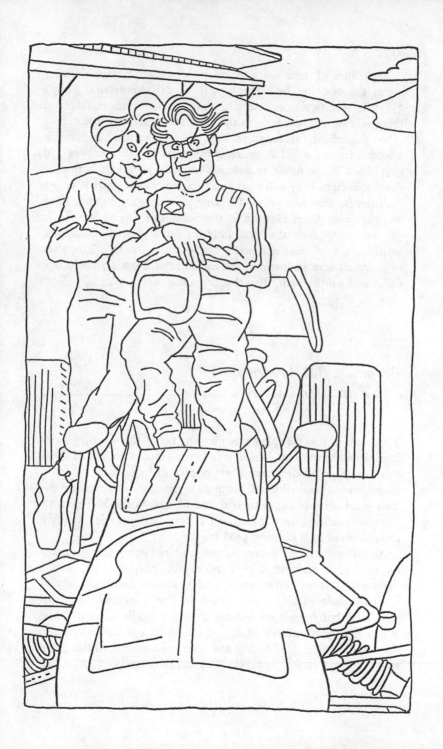

Regardless of your track position, you should start thinking about the two hundred laps you'll be driving around Indy's 2½-mile rectangular course. On that fateful Sunday afternoon there will be 150,000 fans in the stands and another 100,000 or so on the infield (although perhaps the best view of the race is afforded from the V.I.P. suites above turn 2). Jim Nabors will sing "Back Home Again in Indiana" and the president of the Indianapolis Speedway will start the race. For many years it began with the familiar sentence: "Gentlemen, start your engines," but in 1977 (with Janet Guthrie in the field) this was amended to: "In company with the first lady to qualify at Indianapolis, gentlemen, start your engines." The engines heat up. You start to move, as does each car in the eleven rows. First a parade lap, followed by a pace lap, then the green flag, and you're off!

Become a Bat Boy for the San Francisco Giants

There are so many adolescents growing up in this country looking for decent summer jobs that it seems a shame so few of them can have that oft-dreamed-of experience of being bat boy for a major league baseball team. Imagine a youngster fifteen to seventeen years old rubbing mitts with the likes of Willie McCovey or John Montefusco, seeing baseball history being made, hanging around his idols, and being paid for it.

About half a dozen young people are hired every year on every major league club to take care of the players' bats, to be "gophers" (go for coffee, etc.), and to absorb the diplomacy of baseball while earning pin money. In San Francisco the man who hires bat boys is equipment manager Eddie Logan. Eddie is proud to be a member of one of the oldest baseball families in the major leagues (his family has been connected with the game since the turn of the century). The bat boys are paid about ten dollars a day for every day they work, and at the end of the season the players usually contribute twenty dollars each as a bonus that is divided among the batboys. Logan has 1,000 letters on file from adolescents all over America. Some of the letters are from kids no older than ten but eager to get their names on the waiting list early. Actually, there is no waiting list, simply a steady turnover of boys who generally work until they're old enough to go to college. Usually the new bat boys have been recommended by the old ones, or by someone already in baseball. It's best to write to every club, telling them you're willing to travel. You may want to contact a minor league club, pick up some experience, and see if you can gain an entree that way. Eddie Logan hires a few bat boys and a few ball boys (Oakland has ball girls who run down foul balls) each year, and keeps one or two "on the line," or ready to step in if the occasion arises.

If you get the job, here's what you'll be doing:

getting sandwiches for the players, putting their bats out on the bench, helping put the fresh uniforms around the clubhouse, and listening to the players when they want to talk. The senior bat boy will usually be the one to help prepare the umpires' room, unpack their bags, shine their shoes, and take care of their laundry. The fun part of the job is the opportunity to shag flies in the outfield during batting practice, and, once in a great while, getting a chance to break into baseball.

If you don't want to be a bat boy, Eddie Logan and every other equipment manager in the majors can think of a thousand kids who'd love it.

Compete for the Title of Miss Rodeo America

Each December cowgirls from all over the United States mosey on down to Oklahoma City hoping to corral the title of Miss Rodeo America. Organized in 1955 for the purpose of promoting

professional rodeo, the Miss Rodeo America contest is in the market not just for a pretty face but for a girl who exhibits excellent horsemanship, a good personality, and, uh, a pretty face.

Sponsored by a variety of rodeo organizations, this pageant offers something to strive for to girls whose home is where their horse is. Judges are on the lookout for the girl who best personifies the ideal Western-type American girl. This past year, contestants represented more than forty states and two Canadian provinces.

Each of the contestants is interviewed by a panel of judges and then given a chance to show her horsemanship at the State Fair Arena. The girls draw for mounts (they ride horses that are strange to them: rules will not allow them to bring their own horses), and then each contestant circles the stadium cowboy style, which means at least a hard gallop and often a dead run. This is done while each girl waves and smiles to the audience. It's not easy, and accidents sometimes happen, but these girls are experienced riders. One of the liveliest events in the competition is goat-busting. Some goats refuse to be thrown and have the annoying habit of lying down just as they are approached. The rules require that each girl "throw" a goat, not just pounce on him when he's down, so occasionally a sturdier goat must be found to replace a cowardly one.

Finally, after several more days of interviewing, competitions, dinners, and other festivities, the winners are chosen. The winner and first five runners-up receive several thousand dollars' worth of scholarships. All of the girls are showered with hats, boots, Western outfits, halters, saddles, and other riding gear. Miss Rodeo America does not necessarily go on to future contests, but to getting back in the saddle again and riding off into the sunset.

ARTS AND ENTERTAINMENT

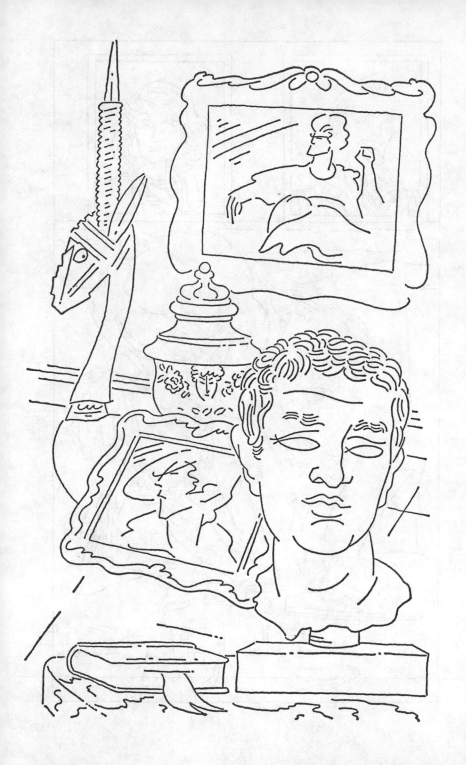

Have a Caricature of Yourself
Hang on the Walls of Sardi's _____

The gastronomic center of the Broadway theatre district is Sardi's Restaurant. Countless performers have chewed their fingernails instead of their cannelloni while awaiting the verdict of the *Times* drama critic. Theatre parties have lunched there as a ritual prelude to myriad Wednesday and Saturday matinees. Films have been shot there, and unknowns have become knowns while enjoying a portion of Sardi's osso buco.

You know you've got it made when a caricature of you hangs on Sardi's walls. It's not just that you opened that week in a big hit or that you know Mr. Sardi: you have to have arrived, solidified your reputation. Here's how this clever gimmick grew into a tradition:

In the early 1930s, Irving Hoffman, a press agent, brought a talented caricaturist, Alex Gard, to lunch at Sardi's. They sat at a large table with a group of regular customers. Gard drew some caricatures of his fellow diners, and, for fun, they stuck them on the walls. The idea became so popular that Gard continued doing caricatures in exchange for two meals a day. He got through the Depression, eventually earned a fee for his caricatures, and kept doing them until 1947. Don Bevan continued the tradition, until recently, when Richard Baratz was hired as caricaturist. Most of Gard's early caricatures are now part of the Lincoln Center Library of the Performing Arts' permanent collection.

At one time, to have your caricature on the walls of Sardi's, you had to be a dramatic actor. Eventually, musical comedy stars were included. Still later, boxers like Carnera, Dempsey, and Tunney were framed. Today, caricatures of well-known people from all areas of sports, politics, and show business grace the walls. About 400 caricatures hang on Sardi's walls at any one time, and their positions change frequently when they are taken down for cleaning. The only ones that do not change positions are those of Rodgers and Hammerstein (just above table 7) and the ones over the bar: Jackie Gleason, Lindsay and Crouse, "Gentleman" Jimmy Walker, and John Lindsay.

The place of honor is the foyer, where the latest caricatures are on view. If you've recently opened in a show (and your caricature has already been done), it may be temporarily put out in front in honor of your opening. Some people who merit the honor have nixed their pix. Sydney Chaplin didn't want his hung because then "I'd worry about where it would be every time I walked in." He managed to convince Judy Holliday (his co-star in *Bells Are Ringing*) not to have her caricature done either. Mercurial producer David Merrick didn't like his caricature and asked Vincent Sardi, Jr., to take it down (usually the caricatures are hung only after they're signed and sanctioned by the celebrity; Merrick simply tired of seeing himself framed). Woody Allen and Elia Kazan have also politely refused to pose.

Whether one sits in the main dining room or upstairs in the club room, the outstanding celebrities of the past smile down on a new generation of entertainment luminaries, thus lending a touch of immortality to an occupation known for its elusive fame.

Obtain House Seats for Broadway Shows ────

"House seats" are designated seat locations that producers of plays, concerts, and other theatrical attractions put aside for their own personal use or for accommodating special guests of the management. This common theatre practice has been in existence, in one form or another, since ancient times and is practiced not just on Broadway but throughout the nation and the theatrical world. On Broadway, producers often reserve several pairs of house seats at *each performance,* disposing of these seats at their discretion. Occasionally they allot pairs of house seats to key members of the production staff, generally the star performer, author, and director. These seat locations are the same for each performance, and they are, generally, "orchestra center" (which, in theatre parlance, connotes locations between the fourth and twelfth rows in the center section of the orchestra; occasionally, house seats may be on a side section, but then they are generally aisle seats).

Who gets to sit in these choice seats? The press covers the play on the "opening night" and "second night," and they are accommodated with the best available seats for those performances. Following the play's initial performances, tickets for the house seats (which are not passes but are *purchased*) may be earmarked for the producers themselves, their secretaries, friends, members of the show business profession, or less prestigious reviewers; perhaps, also, a V.I.P., who suddenly swoops down on the latest hits, will gobble up house seats. Sometimes, when a play is doing poorly at the box office, even these choice seats go vacant.

How can *you* get house seats? If you are not a blood relative of the producer or a member of the creative team that worked on the show, your best bet is either to find someone who is or to call the show's press agent. He's the one who keeps track of who will fill the house seats (the producer's house seats, at least) at every performance. The producer's house seats are generally used to further the goodwill of the play, accommodating those show business and media people who will probably help spread the good word.

If the show is a big fat hit, forget it: house seats may well be reserved for the next year or two. At early previews of *A Chorus Line*, before it even opened on Broadway, the celebrities included Raquel Welch, Edward Albee, Ingrid Bergman, and Neil Simon. If the play is doing only moderate business, you may, by being polite, enthusiastic about the show, and suitably humble about requesting house seats, be able to secure them for a matinee performance some three or four weeks in the future. After all, the producer doesn't want to be stuck with high-priced seats when the public may not even be filling up the balcony!

There is one tip I can give you, one that may let you avoid the hassles of press agents and feigned humility. Go to the box office about twenty minutes prior to the performance and wait around. Ask the box office manager if there are orchestra seats for that evening's performance. He may very well tell you, "No, but wait around"—because if the producer or press agent was not able to sell the designated house seat locations, they will release the seats to the box office very close to curtain time. The box office manager is then empowered to sell those seats as he would any other seats in the theatre. That's your cue. Tell the box office manager that you are interested in obtaining orchestra center seats and ask him if he anticipates the release of any house seats. If you play your cards right, you'll have a pair of last-minute house seats to a show that may be advertised as being "sold out" for months into the future.

House seat orders are sent by the producer (or his press agent) to the recipient, who in turn presents it at the box office, along with the purchase price of tickets, for tickets at the specified location. The authorization is usually signed by the press agent. The location (e.g., L-1, L-3) refers to two adjacent seats, not in the center section, but on the aisle closest to the center—some people prefer added leg room to being dead center and surrounded by six people on each side.

Practically every theatre is constructed so that the best seats (the ones giving that blend of perfect sight without craning the neck, and far enough back so that the performer's make-up and sweat does not drip on you) are just where any smart producer would want to sit himself: fourth to twelfth row center.

Qualify for an Oscar, Emmy, or Tony Award —

The public slap on the back is a part of American life, and we'd feel cheated if we weren't able to watch the award ceremonies that pay formal homage to our film, television, and theatrical idols. Winning an Oscar, Emmy, or Tony may not always be a sure sign of having given a virtuoso performance, but it does wonders for your reputation, your salability, and your sudden ability to get a decent table at a restaurant.

You can win an Academy Award if you've worked on a film in most any creative capacity during the past year. Ever since 1927 the Motion Picture Academy of Arts and Sciences has been promoting and recognizing excellence in all areas of motion pictures. Today there are 3,300 voting members of the Academy, including directors, actors, producers, exhibitors, distributors, and theatre owners, many of whom gussy up for the presentations. Few of these members are known to the public at large, but they choose the winners whom 75,000,000 people watch on TV every April.

Nominations are decided by panels of judges. Specially qualified judges make recommendations in the more technical areas of the medium (e.g., animation, special effects). The nominations are completed in February and by March 28 the entire Academy votes on the awards. The awards program is presented on nationwide television in April.

Sometimes the awards defy logic: some are used to salve wounded egos or assuage past rebuffs; some are for underdogs; and some reward the skillful art of hype and ballyhoo. Almost everything from politics to hair styles to gossip influences the awards. To increase your chances, try to work on a film that has a low budget (like *Rocky*), an important message (like *Network*), is taken from a popular novel (like *Godfather*), and stars Robert Redford (like *All the President's Men*). Also, make sure that release of your film is timed to allow your voting members enough time to appreciate it and not enough time to forget about it. Talk up the film, and have your agent talk about your role in making it a success. Steal a scene if you have to. Let it be known that you won't attend the ceremony because you (a) don't believe in awards, (b) are conducting a political protest, or (c) are "on location." When you win, you'll suddenly appear, thank Mom and Dad for their help, and thank "the Academy."

If you last four decades and aren't giving shoe shines on Wilshire Boulevard, you may even get an Irving G. Thalberg

Award (like Pan Berman or Mervyn Le Roy) for meritorious service. In Hollywood, either you can't find work or you're dipped in bronze.

Not to be outdone by motion pictures, television has its own award (the Emmy), its own academy (National Academy of Television Arts and Sciences), and its own byzantine system for rewarding its overachievers. It even has its own schism, because the Los Angeles office has separated from the Academy. Although each chapter of the Academy is free to sponsor its own local awards, the national awards are usually presented in a coast-to-coast televised ceremony.

Every year the television industry is alerted that Emmy nominations are being sought. Everyone in the industry—not just Academy members—is welcome to suggest people and television shows as nominees. A producer may submit the names of people who have worked on his TV programs, but it is also considered good form for an actor or craftsman to nominate himself for an award.

From these entries, ballots are made up and voted on by the nominees' peers (i.e., writers vote for writers, directors for directors, etc.). Price Waterhouse & Company supervises this most complicated of awards procedures and tries to keep everyone honest. Blue ribbon panels comprised of Academy members screen all entries and meet in the middle two weekends in May to select each award winner. Even if the judges are judging a single performance in a particular program, they are obliged to watch the entire program, in each case, before voting.

Daytime TV shows are honored on a program that originates in New York; the nighttime shows are honored on a program that is seen coast to coast and originates in Hollywood.

When Tony Randall won his Emmy his four-word speech was right to the point: "I'm glad I won." But the most telling remark about the Emmys, I think, was Don Meredith's answer to a question about where he keeps his award:

"Right above the washer-dryer."

In New York City the Broadway theatre celebrates itself by passing out Tony awards to the best of its creative artists. The awards are given annually by the American Theatre Wing (which controls the "Tony" name—short for the late actress-producer Antoinette Perry—and receives an annual fee for its use) and the League of New York Theatres. The League of New York Theatres co-ordinates the awards via three committees—administrative, eligibility, and nominating—and the final selection is voted on by 486 theatre people by mail ballot.

The eligibility committee is made up of three people who see every play on Broadway and slot the shows into categories such as "musical," "play," and "revival." They also differentiate the thin distinction between "featured actor" and "actor." The nominating committee—consisting mainly of active theatre reviewers —chooses four nominees in each of the eighteen categories of awards by the first week in May. The awards ceremony is broadcast live from a Broadway theatre in early June. For the past decade this event has been produced by Alexander Cohen and written by his wife, Hildy Parks.

When you hear your name announced as winner, try not to trip on your way to the stage, remember to thank your high school acting teacher, and practice sounding humble. If you lose, take out your photo and résumé and pass it down the aisle.

Have an Actors' Equity Card _____

Actors' Equity Association is the labor union encompassing all professional performers in the legitimate theatre in the United States. The union was founded by 112 actors on May 26, 1913, in New York City. For the twenty years preceding, employers had been encroaching upon the prerogatives of the actors. Exploitation had become a permanent condition of employment and the plight of the actor was becoming increasingly onerous and difficult. There was no standard agreement; each manager drew his own conditions.

Actors' Equity has become a powerful force in the theatre, and it no longer needs new members, in the sense that at almost any given time 80 per cent of Equity members have no jobs in the theatre. In a typical year, 65 per cent of the membership earn less than $2,550. Thirteen per cent have no earnings at all.

Still, there's always someone who wants to "be Equity" and at least be eligible to be cast in a professional production, preferably on the Great White Way. But here's the famous Catch-22: in order to get into the union so that you can get a job, you have to *have* a job. To become a member a person must obtain and present to Equity a standard form of Equity contract signed by a manager, who has agreed to conform to Equity conditions. Thereafter a regular form of application is signed by the prospective member and filed with Equity together with the initiation fee (at the present time $300) and appropriate dues.

Assuming you are a paid-up member for six months of one of the "4A" unions (Associated Actors and Artistes of America), you may join Equity without a contract. A paid-up member of one of these affiliated unions will receive some credit on the initiation fee required by A.E.A. However, if the member joining is in the $25,000-a-year bracket in the entertainment industy, full initiation fees and dues will be required. Should the applicant for membership be an alien, no credit will be allowed for initiation fee or dues to an affiliated union. Dues for alien members are based on 5 per cent of the weekly earnings.

Present your contract, pay your dues, and fill out the application form. When the hurly-burly's done, your credentials will be submitted to Equity and when it is okayed you will be sent a card certifying that you are a member of Actors' Equity Association. Once you're in Equity, you may never again have to play an extra in the eighth bus and truck company of *Hello, Dolly!* in places like Peoria, Ronkonkoma, or Kuala Lumpur.

Win a Pulitzer Prize in Drama _____

Why Marry?, *Miss Lulu Bett*, *The Old Maid*, and *Alison's House*. No, these are not the names of recent pornographic novels or films, they are but a few of the plays and musicals that have won Pulitzer Prizes in drama since the award came into existence in 1917. The Pulitzer has not always been a reliable guide for foretelling which plays will become part of our repertory. Yet the prize, awarded annually by the Board of Trustees of Columbia University and its School of Journalism, has been given to plays by some of our most talented playwrights, including Eugene O'Neill, Tennessee Williams, Arthur Miller, and Edward Albee. A Pulitzer Prize puts you and your play on the map, elevates the play from a "show" to "literature," and doesn't hurt at the box office either.

The Pulitzer in Drama has also had its share of controversy. In 1940, William Saroyan's *The Time of Your Life* won the prize but Saroyan declined it. In 1963 no award was given even though Edward Albee's brilliant *Who's Afraid of Virginia Woolf?* had opened that season (a few members of the Pulitzer jury quit in protest over the decision). Albee's Pulitzer for *A Delicate Balance* (1967) was, it's felt, an attempt to smooth things over and acknowledge Albee's solid reputation. The Pulitzer can also be a jinx, as witnessed by the ups and downs of the careers of Pulitzer Prize-winning dramatists such as Charles Gordone (*No Place to Be Somebody*), Jason Miller (*That Championship Season*), and Howard Sackler (*The Great White Hope*).

Richard T. Baker, secretary of the advisory board, administers the Pulitzer Prizes on behalf of Columbia. The selection of nominees is left up to the board, which takes recommendations from a special jury in drama. The same procedure holds for awards given in journalism, music, the novel, verse, biography, and general non-fiction.

The $1,000 drama prize is drawn from a bequest by Joseph Pulitzer (1847–1911), publisher of the *World*. It is open to professionally produced plays that open during a season lasting from April to March (*The Shadow Box* by Michael Cristofer, the 1977 winner, opened on the last day of eligibility). Prizes are announced in the middle of April.

The advisory board that will review eligible plays is made up of Dr. William J. McGill (president of Columbia University), fourteen journalists, and two Columbia faculty members. If no play of sufficient merit opens, the board can always choose not to make an award. This has happened several times in the past. Musicals are eligible, and some of the past winners have included *South Pacific, Fiorello!* and *A Chorus Line*.

If your play loses out to another, you won't be engaging in sour grapes if you recall to yourself that *The Old Maid* beat Lillian Hellman's *The Children's Hour* in 1934–35, *Harvey* took the award in 1944–45 instead of Tennessee Williams' *The Glass Menagerie*, and the year Arthur Miller's *All My Sons* opened, no Pulitzer was awarded.

Be Appointed Poet Laureate of England _____

If you want a job where the hours are short, the work is steady, and you can really really express yourself, there is one you can pick up for a song . . . or a poem. The person chosen to be poet laureate of England stands as a living symbol of England's past and present contribution to world literature in general and poetry in particular.

In 1616, King James I granted a pension to Ben Jonson, but it was not until 1668 that the laureateship was created as a royal office. Do you have a hankering to be the sage, prophet, and herald of English society? Remember that the position is assigned for a lifetime. The poet laureate is an officer of the sovereign household somewhere beneath Lord Chancellor; his function is to sing the praises of Britain; no heavy lifting required.

There is an opening for the job only when the current poet laureate comes to the end of his own poetic line. Before you can say "onomatopoeia," the Lord Chamberlain officially informs the reigning monarch of the poet laureate's death. In 1967, when John Masefield died after a tenure of thirty-seven years in the position, choosing his successor became a national preoccupation.

The Prime Minister is responsible for putting forth names for a new laureate to be chosen by the sovereign. Many things are considered, such as the preferences of the ruling party, the candidate's attitude toward the monarchy, and English society's attitude toward the candidate. The Royal Arts Committee and the Poetry Society are asked for their recommendations too. The first consideration is that the prospective poet laureate be a good poet (the word "poet" can be taken to mean dramatist also; Nicholas Rowe and Colley Cibber were playwrights who became laureates), but he must also be "acceptable." The press conducts its own search for the proper candidate, and the selection is argued on street corners and in pubs from Piccadilly to Perth.

When a list of eligible poets has been compiled, the monarch sends a formal message to each of them, feeling them out about their views of the laureateship and whether they might be interested should the post be offered to them. This note is the tip-off that they are up for the job, although some snub the honor of being dragged out on state occasions like some Bard-in-the-Box. Masefield accepted the post and wrote practically nothing thereafter; Wordsworth barely managed to write a limerick during the seven years he was poet laureate. The perfunctory character of the laureate's duties often prevents the appointment of the best living poets, though since Wordsworth's time the appointment has with occasional exceptions been regarded as a recognition of poetic distinction.

Now, assuming you're (a) English, (b) a poet, (c) willing to serve, and (d) under consideration, the monarch may well write you (via the P.M.) and offer you the job. If you accept, the Lord Chamberlain will arrange an announcement in the London

Gazette. The pay is negligible, but you might want to do what Sir John Betjeman, the present laureate, does: ask to be paid in cases of wine supplied by the Queen's own wine steward.

. . . or Chosen King of the Mardi Gras ―――――

America loves a parade, and since 1872 one of its favorites has been the Mardi Gras (literally translated as Fat Tuesday) parade, the crowning event of the New Orleans Mardi Gras celebration, the last day before the Lenten season.

The king of Mardi Gras, master of the revel, is chosen by a committee of New Orleans gentry belonging to a mysterious organization known as the Krewe of Rex. No one outside of the Krewe of Rex knows the membership of this committee, and the secrecy that surrounds the king's selection would be a challenge to the C.I.A.—it's airtight all the way. To become a member of the Krewe of Rex, it is helpful if your father was a member and his father before him. Not exactly what you'd call an "open convention," but that's the way it's done in Louisiana.

The man who would be king must be a civic leader in New Orleans, a business or professional man with lots of local popularity. That lucky, lucky man not only reigns over Mardi Gras but gets to wear a gold and silver costume with white boots, a pageboy-style wig, a crown, a scepter, and tons of rhinestones.

On Mardi Gras day he'll ride his float from "Rex Den" (the warehouse that holds the floats) down South Claiborne Avenue, around Canal Street, and down to the River Gate. The route is usually filled with cheering revelers, crushed beer cans, and loads of balloons. The parade doesn't pass through the French Quarter any more because the narrow streets made the parade a fire hazard. In 1978, Edmund McIlhenny was king of the Mardi Gras. Not exactly a household name, but so what? He's the king, and we are just subjects, that is, until the Krewe of Rex meets next year to select another king.

Have Your Photograph Taken by Karsh —————

Don't be surprised if you dial Karsh's New York telephone number and Karsh himself answers the phone. The world-renowned portraitist travels to New York City from his home in Ottawa on the average of once a month, and during those trips he accommodates American clients who have arranged for sittings. What do you need to get a sitting with Yousef Karsh? Cash.

A check will do. Make the check out for $1,000 if you want a single black and white print (an additional 8 by 10-inch print will cost $50, an 11 by 14, $65). Since Karsh usually schedules only two sittings a day, you'll be asked to drop by the studio at either 10 A.M. or about 2:30 P.M. Sittings for color photographs may take a few minutes more, but the print will cost you $1,500, with each additional print priced at $300.

If this monetary montage has made you a bit camera shy, let me remind you of what James MacNeill Whistler said when John Ruskin intimated that Whistler's paintings (which were usually painted in one or two days) were exorbitantly priced: "You are paying," said Whistler, "for a lifetime of sensitivity."

Karsh's brilliant reputation rests not only on fifty years of experience but on his unique ability to evoke the mysterious inner character of his subjects, such as Castro, Shaw, Einstein, John F. Kennedy, Pope John XXIII, Franklin D. Roosevelt, Winston Churchill, and Marilyn Monroe. Karsh loves people, especially people who have an air of mystery about them. He's captured the musicality of Pablo Casals by portraying him, back to the camera, playing his cello. He captured Nikita Khrushchev in a bulky fur coat, and John F. Kennedy with his hands clasped reverentially. Hemingway, looking feisty in a rumpled sweater, suggests the hero of *The Old Man and the Sea.* Perhaps Karsh's greatest triumph was his commanding, poised image of Churchill (he induced Churchill's scowl by snatching the Prime Minister's

cigar from his mouth just prior to snapping the shutter). As one
Karsh client put it, "He could make a roaring lion stand still."

Where should you hang your Karsh photograph? Hang it
where it will be seen by the greatest number of people without
putting it in the center of your living room.

Waltz at the Opera Ball in Vienna _____

In New Orleans, it's the Mardi Gras; in Pasadena, it's the Rose
Parade; in Vienna, the festivity of festivities is the annual Opera
Ball. Held in the auditorium of the state Opera House, this ball
attracts big names, big money, and a cadre of international society and would-be society. You can buy a ticket for only $30, but
of course the really fine places to sit are the boxes. A box for
eight persons costs about $1,500 and some go for as much as
$2,300.

And that's only the beginning of the expense. If you order
French champagne you can expect to pay up to $112 a bottle.
Prosit!

Every year about 7,000 people waltz to the music of a band
made up of members of the Vienna Philharmonic. Some stand
by and eat, gaze, talk, or just pose, hoping that others will be
filled with admiration. Many of the people who come to the ball
do so in order to watch their daughters come out; even U.N.
Secretary-General Waldheim attended the affair when his
daughter made her debut. Many people dine at the world-
renowned Sacher Hotel before attending the ball. The famous
old restaurant, home of the Sacher torte, is just behind the
Opera House, and it features such favorites as venison soup and
beef filet Tallyrand. Sound good?

A few people look upon the Opera Ball as a ludicrous Punch
and Judy show, out of step with the times. Maybe they're right,
but for those who'd like to get a taste of Vienna society, the same
folks who gave you Metternich and Mozart, come on down!

Join the American Society of Composers, Authors and Publishers (ASCAP)

The prestige of some of ASCAP's founders (Victor Herbert, John Philip Sousa, Jerome Kern, and Irving Berlin) has made ASCAP membership an attraction for writers of every type of music imaginable. Joining ASCAP marks you as a professional in a field crowded with amateurs.

A song is just music and lyrics, but when you're in ASCAP it is an annuity as well. ASCAP is not a trade union or a performers' organization but a clearinghouse for performing rights in music. It offers licenses that authorize the public performance of all the music of all its composer, lyricist, and music publishing members. These are valuable rights, and ASCAP collects millions of dollars each year in license fees for its members. All revenues above expenses are regularly distributed to ASCAP members and to affiliated foreign societies.

Richard Rodgers, Sheldon Harnick, Stephen Sondheim, Marvin Hamlisch—there is an endless line of songsmiths who are members of ASCAP. Any composer or lyricist of a copyrighted musical work that has been commercially recorded or regularly published may join ASCAP. A sales copy of the published sheet music or a copy of the commercial recording must be submitted with a signed application form, which is available at ASCAP headquarters in New York.

Associate membership is open to any composer or lyricist who has had one work copyrighted, even if not yet published or recorded. A Copyright Office certificate of registration should accompany the signed application form.

Publisher membership is open to any person or firm actively engaged in the music publishing business and assuming the normal financial risk involved in publishing.

There is no initiation fee. Annual dues are currently $10 for writers and $50 for publishers.

If you ever do write a popular song, one that becomes a standard, you and your heirs may look forward to a lifetime of ASCAP royalties. Someday you may even see your name in the ASCAP biographical dictionary. This 845-page hard-cover book contains biographical sketches of writer members and a list of all publisher members. When you're in the book, you'll rest easy knowing that each time you hear your song performed—in restaurants, on television, on the radio—your fortune has increased without your lifting a finger.

Have Your Name on the League of New York Theatres' Opening Night List _____

It's fun to see a play before the critics have reviewed it, and even more fun to see it on opening night, when the performers are concerned about the all-important first impression. The critics are automatically invited to the opening because of what is known as the opening night list. The list is made up by press agents associated with the League of New York Theatres and it guides producers in their decision as to who should review the play.

To be included on the first night list, you must represent a newspaper, magazine, radio station, or television network, and you must be located in metropolitan New York. Naturally the critics from the New York *Times,* New York *Post,* New York *News, Wall Street Journal, Time,* and *Newsweek* are on the list, but not everyone who attends the opening is on the list. You may find yourself invited to the opening if you've put money in the show or if you have a friend in the cast or are related to the set designer, costume designer, or box office manager.

The formal list changes from year to year because the burden of three or four openings a week during the season is often enough to do in even the most stage-struck of reviewers. Every year a committee of eight press agents meet to refine the list, remove the names of reviewers who have not been showing up (or have been giving their seats away), and discuss the credentials submitted from reviewers representing new or upcoming media. The press agents want to keep out the opportunists and culture vultures while keeping in those who can do the shows some good.

Your best bet for being invited is to occasionally request seats for the second night. A second night list, drawn up to accommodate people from the media whose newspapers and magazines are smaller or less prestigious than those of the people attending the opening night, is easier to crack. Here's your opportunity to write a piece for your neighborhood paper (or even an out-of-town paper) by directly requesting second night seats from the play's press agent. Since many second-nighters are particular about which shows they review, sometimes a second-nighter will return seats to shows that were not well reviewed the evening before. At that time an amateur writer can try to convince a press agent that it would be good for the play if he wrote a review for his local paper. You might try to line up an assignment to review a particular play and then call the press agent (or write on letterhead) requesting second night seats. If you can write a persuasive letter, you may well get your two complimentary seats. When your review of the play appears, send a copy to the press agent (especially if it's a good review) along with a letter of thanks. That way you'll build good will, work your way up to a permanent spot on the second night list, and, from there, take aim on the opening night list.

Become a Member of the American Academy and Institute of Arts and Letters ─────────────

In the race for artistic academies, France has the lead but the United States is gaining rapidly. The American Academy recently merged with the Institute of Arts and Letters, and the result is a conglomeration of societies that point the way for all Americans engaged in the arts. The Institute has 250 members (89 in art, 121 in literature, and 40 in music), and vacancies occur only by death. The arts section of the Institute is open to painters, sculptors, graphic artists, and architects. The literature section welcomes novelists, dramatists, essayists, critics, historians, philosophers, and "creative" journalists (e.g., the late Walter Lippmann). Vacancies in the music section can be filled only by composers.

When vacancies occur in a particular section of the Institute, they are filled by annual election. Nominations to fill the vacancies emanate from the particular department requiring a replacement. Nominations are proposed and must be seconded by two people. A departmental ballot is prepared, and the department whittles down the list to a certain number of names that appear on a postal ballot mailed to the entire membership of the Institute. Those nominees receiving the most votes are the first in line to vacancies within the appropriate departments. Once you've joined the in crowd, you then have the prestigious task of conferring fellowships and scholarships on upcoming artists, writers, and composers, as well as granting various medals for distinguished service in the various arts.

The Academy—50 members elected from the membership of the Institute—further honors the most deserving members of the Institute. When you are elected to the Academy you have "ar-

rived," and you can converse with Katherine Anne Porter, Lillian Hellman, or Andrew Wyeth as an equal. It means that you have attained a plateau in the profession above the regional cabals and local literary mafiosi. Academy members are the only ones who vote for those who will join them in that charmed circle. Currently, poet Richard Wilbur is the Chancellor of the Academy.

So many of us grow up wanting to be artists, writers, or musicians and instead become milkmen, furriers, and landlords. It's comforting to know that at the American Academy and Institute of the Arts a few living artists are being put on a pedestal that won't be shaken by the vicissitudes of gossip, bad reviews, or other vagaries usually associated with mortality.

Reserve a Date to See the Barnes (Art) Collection

Dr. Albert C. Barnes was no fool. While Philadelphians were ridiculing exhibitions of French Impressionists, Barnes was acquiring the canvases of Cézanne and Renoir as fast as he could write checks. No wonder that, when Barnes chartered his collection in 1927 as an educational institution, he wasn't eager to share his treasure with fellow Philadelphians. However, since the city was helping share the tax load of the Barnes Foundation, the courts ruled, in 1951, that the public should have access to Barnes's multimillion-dollar collection.

And here's the access they were—and are—permitted: Fridays and Saturdays (9:30 A.M. to 4:30 P.M.). Advance reservations are advisable and are limited to 100 people each day. On Sundays (1 P.M. to 4:30 P.M.), only 50 advance reservations are accepted. You may get in if you show up without a reservation since a limited number of people may enter on a rotating basis (e.g., when five leave, five more may enter), but if the line is long you might be disappointed. There is a certain cachet about knowing of the Barnes Collection and having the foresight to reserve ahead. Remember that the collection is closed to the public during July and August.

Is the Barnes Collection worth a trip to the environs of Philadelphia? It is to people who don't want to miss seeing the 65 Renoirs, more than a hundred Cézannes, a Goya, a Delacroix, and treasures of Egyptian, Persian, Chinese, and Hindu art. An added bonus is Matisse's *The Joy of Life*, probably the most important painting of his long career.

You may call the Barnes Foundation for a reservation, but reserve by mail if your group is larger than eight. Be prepared to suggest alternate dates should the date you request be completely booked. The very first gallery you enter will convince you that all the roadblocks were worth overcoming. It contains Cézanne's brilliant *Cardplayers* and about 20 Renoirs, and some humorless guards who won't let you get close enough to the *Cardplayers* to do any kibitzing.

Judge the Cannes Film Festival _____

The Cannes Film Festival is organized madness. More than 21,000 credentials were given out to actors, producers, directors, distributors, and motion picture executives in 1978. The festival lured people from the Middle and Far East, as well as New York, London, Paris, and Berlin. More than 40,000 attended and watched the 26 films that were part of the festival, not to mention the *Marche*, dozens of films that are screened outside the festival itself. Many go to play tennis, to look at the bikini-clad starlets posing on the gravel beaches, or to visit the casino. The

judges go to see the films, award the prizes, and add a bit of dignity to the proceedings.

Do you picture yourself walking on the Croisette with Lauren Hutton, Curt Jurgens, Roger Moore, Sophia Loren, and Albert Finney? You can try to get an assignment to cover the festival from your newspaper, but of course you'll probably have to pay your own expenses (1,270 French and foreign journalists were accredited in 1977). But if you want to be a judge, you don't stand a chance unless you are either (1) a celebrated critic, film star, or director or (2) a part of the French film industry hierarchy. If you want to know who has judged or will be judges for the next festival, drop a letter to Maurice Bessy, the Delegate-General of the Cannes Film Festival.

The nineteen-member jury must see 26 films in fourteen days (they are checked in and out of screenings). Critics like Rex Reed and Pauline Kael jam the Palais des Festivals theatre, see the films, check their notes, rush off to the next screening, attend press conferences, and are instructed not to order à la carte. Even if you're not called on to be a judge, it's fun to stand back and observe this festival, which has become a three-ring circus. Watch the businessmen turning somersaults to close film deals over Perrier water at the Majestic Hotel, directors exposing their films to bleary-eyed judges, and photographers in a Keystone Kops chase scene snapping anything in a swim suit that moves.

Be a Supernumerary at the Metropolitan Opera

It may sound super to be a supernumerary at the Metropolitan Opera, but the hours are long and the pay is barely enough to cover subway fare. Supernumeraries—walk-ons, who walk on stage without speaking lines or as part of a crowd—seek the job because they love opera, want stage experience, or are just plain stage-struck. There are students from Columbia holding spears in *Aida*, and they may well be standing next to businessmen who have never been on stage before or professionals at liberty between parts. A lot depends on your physical type and how that compares with the particular opera being cast. For a production of *Hansel and Gretel*, the assistant stage manager in charge of supers hired ballet students from a school in New Jersey. When muscular types were needed, he went to a high school and persuaded the wrestling team to be a part of the cast. Obviously an operatic voice is not a requirement.

Find out what operas are being planned and ask when supers are being hired. If you're physically right, you may get a part. Then you'll show up for rehearsals, appear in perhaps seven performances over a two- or three-week period, and get transportation, a meal and be paid a nominal salary ($4.00 usually).

If you've had stage experience, bravo; but you must never sing on stage. Just do what you're told and don't drop anything. Cooperate, and you stand a better chance of becoming a regular.

If you have a special skill, you may also get special consideration. Are you a good enough acrobat to do a few random cartwheels in *Pagliacci?* Even if your chief asset is that you are a warm body, there may be a walk-on or march-on role for you in Berlioz' *Trojans* or that old boon to employment, *Aida.*

The New York season runs from October to April and then the Met goes on tour, so if you're persistent you may get a chance to be on stage even if you don't live in New York. All of the inconvenience and the temptation to sing when you're not supposed to will not dissuade operatic die-hards from the thrill of taking a bow a few short feet from the most gifted singers of our era.

Make a Guest Appearance on the Tonight Show ————————————

There is no one method or system for selecting guests on the Tonight Show. The show has five talent co-ordinators whose job it is to research, hire, and arrange for the guests who appear nightly (11:30 P.M. E.S.T. on NBC—although the show has been taped at 5:30 P.M. Pacific Standard Time to be run that evening).

Generally speaking, agents and business managers of particular celebrities may contact the Tonight Show and let them know of the availability of a star or performer whom they represent. Sometimes it is the Tonight Show co-ordinators who seek out particular people who are in the news for one reason or another. The co-ordinators get some of their ideas for guests by poring over local newspapers to discover off-beat people with special talents or people who have done unique things. When they decide to inquire into a future guest's availability, they'll usually call him and, if he wants to be on the show, offer to fly him out to California.

There is a production meeting every morning during which the staff decides the line-up of the scheduled guests. If there is a cancellation, substitutes are drawn from an availability list. Cancellations are not common, but the staff still prefers to book people for the show as far as six weeks in advance.

The Tonight Show is always interested in discovering new talent, and they're pleased to have young comics submit video cassettes of themselves in action or have a singer send in a résumé of where he or she has appeared. Every night three to six guests join Johnny, and they're scheduled along with the occasional visits from members of the Carson repertory: "Carnac

the Magnificent," "Aunt Blabby," or "The Mighty Carson Art Players."

As the guests get ready to go on, waiting in the greenroom of the NBC Studio in Burbank, Carson or Ed McMahon may drop by to give them a few words of encouragement. Just before the taping begins, Ed McMahon comes out to warm up the studio audience. And at 5:30 P.M. the strains of Paul Anka's "Theme" of the Tonight Show is played by Doc Severinson and the NBC band, while McMahon announces the guests. After Carson completes his five-minute monologue, it's time for the guests to get their acts together. Then the talent co-ordinators start worrying about the next day's show. They must be doing something right: the Tonight Show has been going strong for more than fifteen years and has presented more than 14,000 guests to audiences averaging 9,000,000 home viewers.

CLUBS AND ASSOCIATIONS

Have a Listing in the
Social Register _____

Who gets a listing in the *Social Register?* Obviously that is Highly Privileged Information, because if you call the *Social Register* office you'll find a reluctance to impart information matched only by that of the K.G.B., box office managers, or presidential press secretaries. New people keep getting in as the *Register* is updated regularly with new listings of births, deaths, and marriages.

To be listed in the *Register,* you must be proposed by someone who is already listed (which, of course, leads to the question of how the first listee got in; immaculate conception, perhaps). The person proposing your name should state some specific details about your life, your family, schools attended, spouse's family, children, marital status, children's ages, clubs, associations, and other things of grave importance. Next, you'll need five letters of recommendation. These letters can be from clergymen, politicians, or businessmen, but all of the people doing the recommending must already be listed in the *Social Register.* An advisory board looks over your credentials and decides whether your blood is blue or just a shade of green. The *Social Register* plays by its own rules, and no one ever finds out just why he or she was not anointed.

It is an automatic courtesy to list the President of the United States, and the Carters are included, along with listings of the Carters' three adult sons and their wives. Those of us who would rather not run the country will have to earn our listings the hard way.

Join the Explorers' Club . . . ─────────────

If each of us has only sixty or seventy years on earth, we might as well spend them poking around a bit. Each generation spawns individuals who wonder what is just beyond the horizon, and who spend their lives taking trips to places that have never graced a map. There is an elite fraternity for explorers who find fellowship, story swapping, and lectures an impetus for joining.

Located at 46 East 70th Street, New York City, the Explorers' Club boasts a world-wide membership of more than 17,000.

The club was founded at the turn of the century by Henry Collins Walsh (along with 50 others) "to bring explorers together to promote further exploration and to have a good time." Into the oak-paneled entrance room, main-floor sitting room, and fifth-floor trophy room have sauntered men and women with track records of notable scientific research and world travel, people such as Theodore Roosevelt, William O. Douglas, and Edmund Hillary. The club's world-renowned library, on the third floor, contains more than 20,000 books, maps, and documents pertaining to exploration.

To join, you need to have two present members willing to sponsor your membership. New members must have a substantial body of research behind them and must be "actively engaged in increasing man's knowledge of the world."

Then you can get in on the delicious foods served at the annual Explorers' Club dinner—reindeer sausage, moose meat balls . . . roast lion . . . marinated boar . . . and red sheep roast. I'll let the desserts be a surprise.

. . . or the Friars . . . ————————————————

One myth that pervades the all-male Friars Club, the society of international entertainment personalities, is that you have to be a big star in order to join. Not true at all.

There are two categories of membership: professional and non-professional. Professional membership (two thirds of the club's members are "professional") requires that at least 75 per cent of an applicant's income be derived from the entertainment field. All new members must be proposed and seconded by friends who are already members of the Friars. An application will then be furnished to the prospective member, asking details about his occupation, associations, and bank references. At the bottom of the application the "proposer" and "seconder" may write a few words on the applicant's behalf. By the way, the initiation fee ($300) and the yearly dues ($550) are payable in advance.

Once you're in, there is a garden of earthly delights for you to partake in—fine dining rooms, swanky bars, a health club, reading room, billiard room, and barbershop, plus companionship with the tops in the theatrical profession. It's men only at lunch (the Friars is a men's club) but women are welcomed to the Friars during evening activities and dinner.

Members are not only permitted to vote on club business but are also welcome to attend the "Roasts" (lunches) which occur biannually. They are also privileged to attend the annual testimonial dinner (in 1978, David Brinkley, Walter Cronkite, and Howard K. Smith were honored). Aside from testimonial dinners and roasts, the Friars do a great deal of charitable work for which they receive little publicity. Recently, they established the Friars Foundation, which raises funds to support the arts. Every Christmas the Friars collect toys and clothes which they distribute to hospitals and foundling homes throughout the community.

The Friars is a nirvana for name-droppers since its officers include Frank Sinatra, Milton Berle, and Red Buttons. Some officers have special designations: for example, Frank Sinatra has been elected Abbot. Johnny Carson (Knight), Paul Anka (Herald), and Sammy Davis, Jr. (Bard), and Alan King (also a Herald) are just a few of the specially appointed officers. The "Dean" is Buddy Howe, former president of International Creative Management, titular head of the Friars, and in charge of its day-to-day operation. The Friars may sound like a monastic organization, but it's anything but cloistered.

. . . or the Mayflower Society

How far back can you trace your roots? To the Civil War? To the Revolutionary War? Why not go the whole hog and see if anyone in your distant past had a bunk on the *Mayflower*? If your ancestors weren't on board, perhaps they were wait-listed.

The Mayflower Society is like the Daughters of the American Revolution except that (1) you don't have to be a woman to join, and (2) the Mayflower Society expects you will be able to trace your family back to that historic boat ride of 1620. If you can prove that your lineage goes back to one of the *Mayflower*'s passengers—using family genealogies, wills, deeds, cemetery records, or old Bibles—you probably will have no trouble becoming a member.

When you submit your papers, they'll be scrutinized with care. After all, just as *everybody* claims to have seen Babe Ruth's "called shot" home run in 1932, and *everyone* claims they were in the opening night audience of *My Fair Lady*, everyone feels that, somewhere along the line, they are descended from those brave Massachusetts Pilgrims. Actually, there were only 102 pas-

sengers on the *Mayflower*, and half of them died the first year in the New World. Many of the survivors were forced to intermarry just to keep the population up. Mayflower Society members are canny, and they check their *Mayflower Index* carefully—anyone whose name has ever been used in establishing lineage to the *Mayflower* is listed in that book. Another source they turn to is *The Truth About the Pilgrims*, which gives a history of each one of the *Mayflower*'s passengers and also discusses some of their more famous descendants. Churchill was a member of the Mayflower Society (via his mother's family); Franklin Roosevelt was eligible for membership but he never joined. Nelson Rockefeller is one of the most illustrious present members of the society.

When you do get to be a member you'll do such things as plan the annual Mayflower Ball. The first Friday of each November is the date for this gala affair, which features the "coming out" parties of the daughters and granddaughters of the members. The money derived from this affair goes into the Mayflower Fund, which helps provide aid for needy students.

Every three years delegates from each state's Mayflower Society journey to Plymouth to make policy for the next three years. One delegate for each twenty members attends the conference. What else is there to do in Plymouth?

Audition for the Mormon Tabernacle Choir ___

In order to be a good Mormon, you have to give up coffee, tea, smoking, loose morals, and a tenth of your gross income. If you think that's difficult, it's just openers if you want to become a member of the Mormon Tabernacle Choir.

You may apply to the Mormon Tabernacle Choir if you can get your home-town bishop to write a letter in your behalf, certifying that you are following the Mormon Word of Wisdom, that you are active in your ward (parish), and that you live a good, clean life. An appointment will be arranged for you to take a written test on musical theory. In it, you will be asked to recognize types of minor keys, differentiate correct from incorrect rhythm, know your key signatures, spot augmented and diminished chords, and recognize intervals by both hearing and seeing them in print. A score of 60 per cent is required in order for you to move to square two: the vocal audition.

In the vocal auditions, which are held each year in January, April, July, and September, you will be asked to match tones, repeat, from memory, a few unusual note groupings, do some sight reading (with and without accompaniment), and sing a hymn with accompaniment and also *a cappella*.

Your audition will be graded by Jerold D. Ottley, director of the Mormon Tabernacle Choir, and his associates. You'll be judged on your voice: pitch, rhythm, and quality. Your theory test and audition are appraised on a rating sheet that produces a raw score. If your raw score is between 50 and 59, you are "3"; if you score between 60 and 74, you are "2"; and if you score between 75 and 100, you are graded "1." Only those scoring "1" are considered for membership in the choir. Others are sent letters encouraging them to try again and to work on their musical weaknesses.

If you are chosen to be one of the nearly 400 singers who perform in the choir, you will have to commit yourself to at least an 80 per cent attendance record at the Tabernacle (usually Thursday evenings and Sunday mornings) as well as make yourself available for tours (usually one two-week tour annually) and recording sessions. No one is permitted to remain in the choir longer than twenty years, and retirement age is sixty. Of course, as with any choir group, your services are given on a strictly voluntary basis.

Being in the choir isn't bad, but some may object to those coffeeless coffee breaks. . . .

Become a Member of Mensa

Are you a part of America's intellectual elite? Do you read Kafka and Kant the way some people read comic books? If you happen to be among the top 2 per cent of the nation in intelligence, you qualify to join Mensa. Mensa (the Latin word for "table," signifying a round table of equals) has three activities as an organization: to conduct research in psychology and social science, to identify and foster human intelligence, and to promote social contact among its members. Unofficially, Mensa membership can be an interesting conversation piece or party icebreaker, and it can provide you with some well-placed contacts in the academic, scientific, and business establishment.

Would you like to join? Don't be shy about your intelligence, that's the first thing to remember. If you write to Mensa, they'll be happy to send you a "take home" examination (cost: $6.00) that will test the sort of perceptions one can't look up in the family Britannica (e.g., If John is three years older than Matilda, and Matilda is six years older than Mortimer . . .). Assuming you pass this preliminary test, you'll be invited to take a proctored examination (cost: $15), usually given once a month in most major cities.

The three-and-a-half-hour examination tests your native intelligence by presenting puzzling problems in mathematics, verbal acuity, reasoning, and spatial relationships. The best way to hedge your bet is to take any and all other IQ tests that come your way through life—College Boards, Graduate Record Examinations, Army General Classification Tests, Law Boards—because Mensa will accept you if you've ranked in the top 2 per cent of those taking any of the previously mentioned tests. Even the Mensa examination consists of two separate tests, and you need to qualify only on the result of either test.

It's nice to be able to qualify for Mensa, whether you wish to join or not. The great advantage of joining is not simply the éclat of achievement or the pride in your mother's heart. It is making social, business, and, yes, even spiritul contact with those people—Isaac Asimov, Theodore Bikel, and Buckminster Fuller among them—who are proud of what Mensa stands for and not ashamed to be brainy.

Gain Admittance to a Nudist Camp _____

If you never seem to get a "Cheer" wash, never have "a thing to wear," or if your department store never has your size, you may want to consider taking up nudism.

The American Sunbathers Association consists of members who have joined by associating themselves with local nudist clubs and camps. Nudists are not zealots, they are people who literally and figuratively let it all hang out.

To get into a nudist camp, simply camp at its doorstep and request membership. They'll take a long look at you and try to determine whether you see nudism as a healthy, natural thing or whether you're doing it for a quick pickup. Nudist clubs range from facilities that operate all-year round (mostly in the South, of course), to others with overnight accommodations. A few don't have any facilities for overnight camping: these are day camps, to coin a phrase. Each winter one nudist camp in New Jersey has a sign on its locked front gate that reads "Clothed for the winter."

How old do you have to be to join? Oh, about one day old is the minimum age, and the maximum age is well up past ninety. Generally, it is easier for couples to be accepted than singles (private clubs set their own membership requirements), and easier for single women to join than it is for single men. Nudist clubs try to strike a balance in their membership. That way,

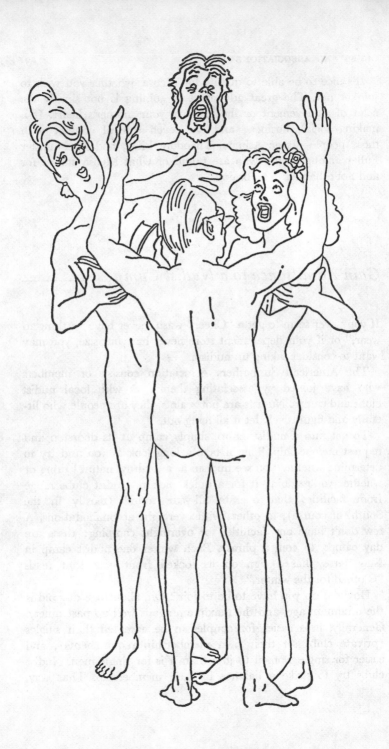

families don't become upset and the campgrounds don't come to resemble a sunshine-filled singles bar. If a club is co-operatively owned, a panel of members will decide on your membership.

If you just want to visit a nudist camp, that's all right too. Although rules vary from club to club, you may well be permitted one or two free visits. Most clubs will ask men to disrobe completely, but women may opt to keep one or two garments on. At many clubs there are pools, lakes, ponds, volley ball games, clubhouses, and a generally relaxed feeling of good-fellowship. The rules that apply to conduct in a nudist camp are, in a way, similar to those that would apply in most church groups.

Nudist camps have come a long way since the paranoia of "a pervert under every bush" pre-sexual revolution hysteria. With nude bathing, braless high school girls, and the general loosening of sexual prohibitions in society, nudist camps have a benign, almost quaint connotation. Anyone who behaves is welcome (i.e., leave your binoculars at home).

MISCELLANEOUS

Visit China

If you just want to touch your toes on Mainland China's soil, you can always book passage on the *QE II*. Their round-the-world cruise is bound to give you a day or two in Canton, with braver shipmates finding their way to Peking and the Forbidden City. Peking accepts cruise tours only on a year-to-year basis, so there is no guarantee that next year China won't be closed for (political) alterations. Besides, the *QE II* and other cruise ships are an expensive way to get to see Shanghai, Whampoa, and scenic Kweilin.

By now, everyone knows that you have to be invited to visit China, and that you have to undergo a somewhat rigorous process of application, and that the chances are that you'll still be turned down for a visa. The Chinese put out the welcome mat to Americans who have what they feel is a legitimate reason for seeing China (a craving for authentic Peking duck is considered insufficient reason to issue a visa). The Chinese favor Americans who are interested in some aspect of contemporary Chinese society (such as medicine or education). Other things that may help you win acceptance are a Chinese ancestry or a background in some scientific or technical field about which the Chinese feel you could be helpful. A sympathy for their revolutionary cause also gains favor. Yet Peking has rebuffed some scholars with the stern warning that further visits must await normalization of relations between the United States and China. For the latest information about the arrangements for visiting groups of scholars, check with the Committee on Scholarly Communication with China (Washington, D.C.).

Group visits are easier to arrange than individual visas. You might start by requesting an invitation from the China International Travel Service (Luxingshe), Xitan Building, East Changan Street, Peking, People's Republic of China. Write in English, and explain what you hope to see and do (your concern should be with *today's* China, not with historical artifacts). You should include a short biography of everyone in your group (mention specific affiliations with diplomatic clout, publications in print, etc.), a statement of how you expect to arrive (by boat from Hong Kong, by air from Manila) and how long you're likely to stay (most visitors stay two to three weeks). If you are friendly with someone who has already been to China, mention it. Another copy of your letter of intention should be sent to the Liaison Office of the People's Republic of China. Should Peking approve your visit, this office will issue your visa (about $5.00).

Two private groups that arrange exchanges and are good sources of information are the National Council for U.S.-China Trade (Washington, D.C.) and the National Committee on U.S.-China Relations (New York). Another organization, the U.S.-China Friendship Society, provides visas for those traveling with its group tours. Most groups will provide you with pamphlets about Chinese customs. Tipping and flirting are definitely *not* done.

If you are invited, make sure that the passport you submit for a visa stamp does not contain a restriction against travel in Mainland China—or a tourist's visa from Taiwan. If you have either, better get a new passport, or you'll be skating on thin rice.

Obtain Permission to Be Married at St. Patrick's Cathedral in New York ⸺⸺⸺⸺

For those who have wished for a big church wedding, holding the ceremony at St. Patrick's Cathedral might seem like the impossible dream. There is something about the cavernous, majestic chapels, the rows of pews, the delicate windows that cries out for ceremonies of enormous dignity and solemnity, yet many regular wedding ceremonies are held at St. Patrick's every year.

The best way to unravel the red tape is to do it a little at a time. Go to the cathedral and make sure that you want to be married there: look it over from a practical as well as spiritual viewpoint. The bride and groom must have parental permission to marry (if under eighteen) and a letter from officials at their home church giving permission for the ceremony to be held at St. Patrick's.

After giving the cathedral's administrative aide a $50 deposit, you will be assigned to a priest who will help you make arrangements and set the date. You have your choice of either the main altar (capacity: 2,000; cost: $225) or the Lady Chapel (holds 80 and costs $175). Either price includes an organist and singer who are hired by the church and whom therefore you are obliged to use. You may select the wedding music, but it must be approved by the priest. Although English is the preferred language, the service can be performed in Latin or almost any other language of your choice.

In what is known as the "pre-marriage investigation," the priest may ask you about your baptism, first communion, and confirmation. You must assure the priest that you never were married before or are free to marry (bring your former spouse's death certificate). If your previous marriage was annulled, legal papers are required. This statement about your marital acceptability, credentials, and accompanying legal verification must be notarized. Are you sure you want to go through with it?

Assuming you haven't backed out or converted to Buddhism by this time, you must also assure the Church that you will try to bring up your children in the faith. This statement must be signed and notarized at least thirty days prior to the ceremony. At least two weeks prior to the ceremony, the banns (announcements) are published in the bride's church stating the couple's intention to marry. This procedure is known as "publishing the banns." It allows all those who might oppose the marriage to speak, or forever hold their respective peace.

Now it's the wedding day, but wait, a few last instructions: no rice or confetti is allowed. A simple bouquet for the bride and flowers at the altar are permissible. No exotic dress, no carpets, and, oh yes, children are not permitted to take part in the ceremony (except to walk up to the altar).

You will, no doubt, be surprised to find that there is usually a six-week waiting list for weekends (Saturdays only: no weddings are performed on Sunday) but during the week you'll be able to get married without taking a number. Where you go on your honeymoon is *your* business.

Be an Extra in a Hollywood Movie _____

During the shooting of a recent film 1,000 citizens of Dubuque, Iowa, were hired at $35 a day to play striking teachers, company goons, and Cleveland cops. An associate professor of music earned a truck driver's part because of his 250-pound frame, but he missed a chance to say one line (and earn $172 extra) when director Norman Jewison decided his hair wasn't quite right. Later, Jewison was so disappointed with the actor playing a cop, he asked him to go find a real cop. The real cop took over the part "as if he'd been doing it all his life."

We may dream of this happening to us, but it usually only happens outside the jurisdiction of the Screen Extras' Guild, or when a producer has already hired at least 175 Guild extras. After 175, the producer may then legally turn to non-union extras (waivers). Of course, there are some non-union production companies and a few Hollywood producers and directors (e.g., Cassavetes, Altman, etc.) who are notorious for using "real people" as extras.

If you have a special skill, you may join the S.E.G. on recommendation from a producer. The casting office with which the film production company is working will help you register with S.E.G. when you're about to be hired.

Although it may seem like status to be an extra in a Hollywood movie, extras have always been on the bottom of the

Hollywood status ladder. Yet the 4,000 members of the S.E.G. are professionals in every sense of the word. They often have their own uniforms and period costumes. They know how to appear in front of a camera, and they often save money for a production company.

Your best chance of being chosen is if a film production comes to your home town, and if your home town happens to be farther than 300 miles from New York, Honolulu, Miami, Las Vegas, Chicago, Hollywood, or the New Mexico-Arizona area. If you live in one of those centers of film (and S.E.G.) activity, better hope that several films start production at once. At one time, when *Rocky* was being shot in Hollywood, so were *Two Minute Warning* and *The Shootist*. The Screen Extras' Guild simply couldn't provide all the extras required by the three productions, so producers were free to hire whom they pleased.

It's at times like this that a producer's neighbors, friends, barber, butcher, and pet cocker spaniel may suddenly find themselves film stars.

Receive the License Plate Designation of Your Choice ——————————————

If you want your initials or three letters of your name on your very own license plate, you need not save box tops or bribe the Commissioner of Motor Vehicles. All you do is request the license plate of your choice. In New York, applicants for special license plates are told that they "may be assigned by the Commissioner to any applicant whose record does not indicate a conviction during the last eighteen months of speeding, reckless or dangerous driving or any offense requiring the revocation of your driver's license. Should you be convicted of such an offense after your special plates are issued, you will not be permitted to renew them." You can obtain a special plate manufactured in most one-, two- or three-letter series. In New York these plates carry an *annual* $5.00 service charge in addition to the regular fee. If your vehicle is currently registered in New York State, special plates may be issued for a fee of $8.25 ($2.00 exchange fee, $5.00 service charge, $1.25 for permanent reflectorized plates). Special plates are not kept in stock. They are ordered upon receipt of Form "S" and a fee. A period of ten weeks is required to manufacture and issue them.

The Department of Motor Vehicles will be happy to send you the proper form. The form will ask for the plate series request, second and third choices, and some information about your present registration. Restaurateur Howard Johnson used to let his license plate advertise his business. His plate read HJ-28.

Stand at the Geographical Center of the U.S.A.

Here's a great vacation idea: seven glorious nights, eight fun-filled days at the geographical center of the United States, somewhere in the buttes of South Dakota. What do you do there? Oh, I didn't know you wanted to *do* anything. It turns out that the middle of the United States is in the middle of nowhere. As a tourist attraction, the center of the United States rates on a par with the Gulag Archipelago.

To get there, start at Rapid City, South Dakota, and, after seeing the Mount Rushmore Memorial and the Badlands, proceed due north along Route 90, which leads to Route 85. After driving about forty miles on Route 85, you'll see a stone marker just off the highway. This marker, located in a quaint part of the prairie, can be found at the top of the overlook. Are you getting excited? Thrill to the knowledge that you are standing at 44 degrees, 58 minutes north latitude; 103 degrees, 46 minutes west longitude. This enchanting spot is located seventeen miles west of

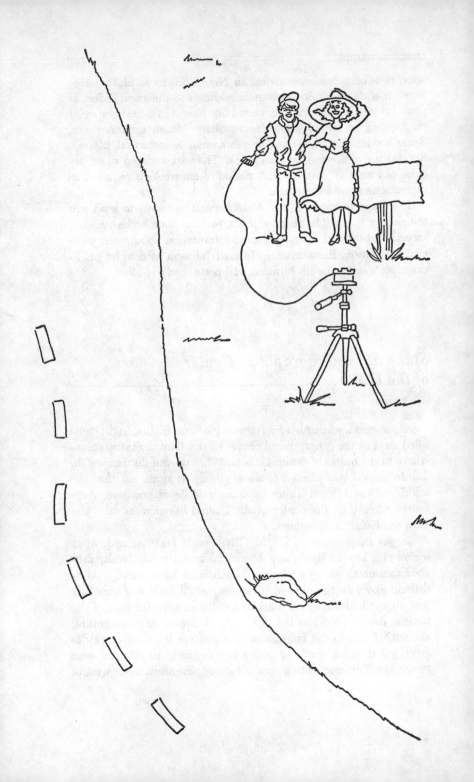

Castle Rock and fourteen miles east of the junction of South Dakota, Montana, and Wyoming. For fun, you can always go to the junction and stand in three states at once.

Kansas was formerly the home state for the geographical center of the forty-eight states. You had to go to Lebanon, Kansas, in Smith County (39 degrees, 50 minutes north latitude; 98 degrees, 35 minutes west longitude) if you wanted to be center stage. In 1959, when Hawaii and Alaska were admitted to the Union, South Dakota inherited this dubious epicentral distinction (although there is no satisfactory way of determining the geographical center, it may be defined as the center of gravity of the surface, or that point on which the surface of the area would balance if it were a plane of uniform thickness).

But if you really want to be surrounded by people, you must travel to Illinois to the *population* center of the United States, about five miles east southeast of Mascoutah, in St. Clair County. If you stand at the exact center, you will be standing at that point upon which the United States would balance if it were a rigid plane without weight and if the population distributed thereon (with each person assumed to have equal weight) exerted influence in proportion to the distance from that point. How about that? Who says that there's "*nothing* to see in the Midwest"?

Participate in the National "Nielsen Survey" of Television Viewing ──────────────────

If you are one of the 1,200 families in America whose television viewing habits are monitored by the A. C. Nielsen Company, a flick of your TV dial may spell doom or delight for each year's crop of new television programs, each hoping to settle into a long, prosperous run. Nielsens also indirectly determine the advertising cost charged to programs' sponsors. Is it any wonder that the Nielsen Company goes to great lengths to assure itself that each family selected for the survey fits accurately into economic, social, and educational categories that will portray the most balanced, typical view of American TV-watching habits? Nielsen is noted for its scrupulousness and accuracy. Is it any wonder that it wishes to keep secret the names of all families whose TV sets contain those notorious "black boxes" (Audimeters) which record on taped cartridges the channels tuned in by all Nielsen families? These tapes form the raw data for the Nielsen reports, which tell, in rating points, how each TV show is doing against its competition.

There's not much you can do about becoming one of the chosen 1,200 families, because Nielsen picks them at random from specially prepared phone books that list people by district. Once a house is wired to transmit the information directly to Nielsen's computer, the house tends to remain in the Nielsen family. If one tenant moves out, the new tenant may well get a letter requesting co-operation in the survey. The letter that the Nielsen Company sends to prospective sample viewers asks no questions about viewing habits or taste but just includes an application that asks for details about income, size of family, and other demographic bits of data. If you're accepted, you get a small box for your TV bearing the words: "TV Serviceman: Please replace Cords and Equipment as You Found Them—A. C. Nielsen Company." You must sign an agreement with Nielsen that you, "both while a member of the panel and for a year after discontinuance of your participation, will not reveal to strangers or people in the entertainment, newspaper, magazine or entertainment business that you are or were a member of our panel." If one show receives a Nielsen rating only one point higher than the competition, it means that 12 more Nielsen families were watching one show rather than the other. If there are 60,000,000 TV families and 1,200 in the sample, each family represents 50,000 households.

For your co-operation, you'll be given an initial fee of $25 and also be paid $25 a month (in cash). Nielsen also picks up the tab for any TV repairs you may need during the year or, if necessary, for a new set. There's a chance you'll be chosen—Nielsen families have a turnover of about 33 per cent annually.

Some people try consciously to affect the ratings by watching only certain shows or certain networks, but most take their responsibilities quite seriously. If your set happens to be on for twenty-four hours in a row, an electronic device that detects a Nielsen-wired set automatically disconnects that set from the main computer. Twenty-four hours of TV watching signals something unusual—even in a TV-mad household—so Nielsen usually will send an agent around to investigate. That way, they determine whether you're ill, or worse, that you aren't being held hostage by an overachieving vice-president of programming.

Patent Your Invention _____

Inventions need patents the way songs need copyrights. Whether you tinker in the garage on Sunday or have aspirations to be the next Morse or Marconi, the first thing to do is get in touch with a patent attorney. The attorney will conduct a "search" to ascertain whether any previous patents exist in the area of your proposed invention. If he finds patents on inventions that seem to be similar to yours, he'll advise you to either drop your idea or get in touch with the patent owner and discuss the possibility of working with him on a refinement of his idea. If no previous patent exists, your lawyer will write what is known as a patent specification, giving the Patent Office a summary of the unique features of your invention. The lawyer submits the specification to the Patent Office and pays a fee dependent on the number of claims made in the specification. Attached to the specification is a statement verifying that you are the sole inventor and that you have no knowledge of another invention of its type, or of any other inventor working along similar lines.

Back at the Patent Office, the specification is assigned to an examiner who again makes a search of patents in your particular field of endeavor. If the second search reveals you as having an idea distinct from all others, an "action" is sent back to your lawyer, requesting modifications in the proposal or an interview with the inventor. If, however, the examiner feels that your invention is not patentable, the patent attorney may take his case to the Board of Appeals.

When it looks as though patent approval is imminent you are allowed to refer to your invention as "Patent Pending," which displays its status as a near patent and discourages would-be plagiarists or other active inventors from claiming a similar patent.

Your patent certificate is a lovely document to behold. It has the seal of the Patent Office and gives a complete description of your patented invention or process. It gives you the right to exclusive assignment of your invention, and the right to exclude others from making, using, or selling your invention throughout the United States. Your patent is valid for seventeen years and may be renewed.

If you have a great idea for an invention, invent it. Additional information about the procedure for obtaining a patent is available from Mr. C. Marshall Dunn, Honorary Commissioner of Patents and Trademarks.

Soon, if you're lucky, you'll be rich and famous, following in the tradition of Thomas Edison, Alexander Graham Bell, and Nathaniel Briggs. In case you're wondering who Nathaniel Briggs is, he's the inventor of a machine that has changed our lives, allowed us to live a brighter existence. Nathaniel Briggs patented the first washing machine in 1797.

Become a Private Investigator _____

Our minds are so conditioned by the escapades of Sherlock Holmes, Jim Rockford, Sam Spade, and other gumshoes that we forget that a private eye's life is more pushing paper than pursuing perpetrators. A modern-day investigator spends as much time

checking up on the fidelity of spouses as he does matching wits with Mafia chieftains. More, in fact.

If you still want the job, get on the telephone to your local Department of Licensing and request information about becoming a private investigator. A person who can convince the Secretary of State (and at least two signers of experience certificates vouching for your experience) that he has been regularly employed in investigative work may get a license. You may want to gather experience by becoming a local sheriff, or a cop with a rank higher than patrolman.[1] Applicants must be twenty-five years of age or over (in New York State) and must be a citizen of the United States. In Illinois a degree in police science or three years' experience as a security guard for an agency are acceptable qualifications for the license.

If a person meets these requirements, he should file an application on a form prescribed by the Department of State which must be accompanied by (1) additional references, as may be required, (2) two photographs of passport size, taken within six months prior to filling out the application, (3) five sets of fingerprints of both hands. Also, applicants are generally expected to submit certificates of approval by not less than five reputable citizens of the community where the applicant resides or transacts business, each of whom certifies that he has personally known the applicant for at least five years prior to the filing of such application and has read the statements in the application and believes them to be true. Certificates of approval must be submitted from persons not related or connected to the applicant by blood or marriage.

If the application is approved by the Secretary of State, the applicant must file a surety bond in the amount of $10,000. (The law imposes additional provisions if the applicant is a firm, partnership, or corporation. In Illinois, the required bond is $5,000.)

Wait: there's more. All future Philip Marlowes must pass a written examination and pay license fees (about $200 every two

[1] For more complete details on the qualification of applicants, check the appropriate pamphlets distributed by your state's Department of Licensing.

years). No license shall be issued to a person convicted of a felony or other misdemeanor unless he has received executive par-
don or a certificate of good conduct from the parole board.

After all the red tape is over, you'll probably find employment
in the toy industry (they hire many private investigators to
secure "top secret" ideas for new toys that are being developed),
the garment industry, or anywhere excessive curiosity is ramp-
ant and information is at a premium.

Have the Telephone Number of Your Choice ___

Have you ever had difficulty remembering a friend's telephone
number? Have you ever had difficulty remembering your *own*
phone number? (Can you remember your own name?)

Don't worry: most of us forget our own phone numbers occasionally. So I guess the best thing to do is to request a phone
number from Ma Bell that is unmistakably your own. Call your
service representative (or your business service rep, in case you're
changing your business phone number), and ask to have your
number changed. Although you can't alter your three-digit exchange, you may want the last four digits of your phone number
to reflect an attitude (1776), a favorite film (2001), or your feel-
ings about yourself (0001). Ask and ye shall receive—provided
that the number isn't already taken by someone else.

Numbers ending in 0000 or even double or triple zero are generally reserved for clients who have multi-line accounts, generally
corporations. Sometimes you can get lucky and have a number
ending in 0, but you probably won't get one ending in 00 without
requesting it. Businessmen often want numbers keyed to their
line of work (NBC's New York phone number is 664-4444, cor-
responding with Channel 4, their local network). Some people
wish phone numbers that are easy to recall because of the position of the digits on the touch-tone phones.

In any case, it will take three business days for you to change your phone number, because computerized sheets must be checked and double-checked, but don't start printing up personal cards or business stationery until the new number is operating. Last-minute foul-ups have been known to occur at the phone company. . . .

Import Your Own Wine Directly from a French Vineyard

Are you the type of person who not only sniffs the wine before tasting it but also sniffs the cork? Are you the type of person who, instead of having visions of sugarplums dance in your head, envisions jeroboams of 1929 Mouton Rothschild, magnums of 1878 Château Lafite, and well-chilled Montrachet?

Picture yourself touring the Champagne region of France, stopping off at various vineyards for a look-see and a taste-smell. Suddenly you taste a champagne that makes Dom Perignon, Piper Heidsieck, and Moët taste like flat ginger ale. Alas, the vineyard is so tiny that its product is not exported to the States. What to do? Simply arrange for it to be sent to you directly. Better order several cases to make it worth while, but cost cannot be considered, or else why would you even think of importing your own wine or champagne in the first place?

The popular châteaux won't let you import their wine, because most of them are already tied to exclusive contracts with major importers, but many small châteaux aren't. So what you have to do upon arriving back in the States is to arrange with a licensed importer or broker to bring in the wine or champagne from the small vineyard of your choice. The agent will arrange to pay the various duties and tariffs.

For example, if you are bringing in wine with an alcohol content of less than 14 per cent, you'll pay seventeen cents a gallon

in federal tax alone; if the wine's alcohol content is more than 14 per cent, you'll pay sixty-seven cents a gallon.

The total cost will vary from state to state. Call your state liquor authority for the exact tax in your state (New York State tax is ten cents a gallon on wine and fifty-three cents a gallon on champagne). What's more, you'll be responsible if any breakage occurs.

Oh, one more worry: the age-old argument as to how well wine or champagne travels. Any wine you import needs an opportunity to "rest" after its long trip. Some retailers forget that wines are, in a way, "alive." They contain bacteria and are in a constant state of change. By letting them sit still for a while after traveling, you'll be encouraging them to come into their own.

Of course, if you live in a place that is "dry"—Evanston, Illinois, for example—you may be looked down on for bringing in liquor anyway. In which case—why are you living there, and have you considered moving?

Recuperate at Walter Reed Army Medical Center

With hospital care at a premium, it's nice to know that there are at least a few Americans who can check into Walter Reed Army Medical Center, one of the finest hospitals in the world, without its costing them a dime. Known for its Executive Branch clientele, this hospital gives people the type of checkup that lets them know exactly how each cell in their bodies is performing.

"Walter Reed," as it is known, is funded by the federal government, and it provides free medical service to active and retired military personnel. If you went to Walter Reed hoping to be admitted and take over one of its 900 beds (10 per cent of which are in private rooms; 30 per cent are in semi-private rooms, the rest in wards), you'd have to be either a military person, a public official, or a civilian emergency.

If you're desperate, you could arrange to catch cold in front of the entrance, in which case you'll be admitted and charged at the rate of $168 a day. If your recuperation will be lengthy, Walter Reed Army Medical Center will try to find another receiving hospital for you.

What many people do not know is that public officials are also allowed to use the facility, after they've been authorized to do so by the Secretary of the Army. Senators, congressmen, and foreign dignitaries may be able to use the hospital's services if they submit a request in writing to the Secretary of the Army, specifying the particular ailments from which they are suffering. They can't just go for a checkup and a lollipop.

Enlisted men who are not currently active do have to pay costs for food, and their dependents may stay at the hospital for a mere $4.10 a day regardless of the care they receive.

Walter Reed Army Medical Center came to public notice during President Eisenhower's recuperations from his two heart attacks. Recently, however, Bethesda Naval Medical Center has become a household word since Presidents Nixon, Kennedy, Ford, and Johnson used its facilities at one time or another. Carter, an Annapolis graduate, will also probably be depending on Bethesda for his medical care. At either Bethesda or Walter Reed, medical care is superb and the price is right.

Earn a Private Pilot's License _____

There's a little Lone Eagle in each of us, some vague yearning to tame the elements of nature whether by flying a kite, sailing a yawl into the wind, or lifting a Piper Cub off a runway. The F.A.A. estimates that there are in America approximately 700,000 non-airline fliers who log about 28,000,000 hours each year flying for business or pleasure. Despite the increasing numbers of student pilots, the licensed pilot is still viewed as a romantic loner, a confident adventurous person who exhibits grace

under pressure. The procedure for qualifying for a private pilot's license is arduous, expensive, and takes up a few pages of F.A.A. regulations, but that just makes it more of a challenge.

Assuming you are at least eighteen years of age, you are expected to accumulate at least thirty-five hours of instruction from a trained flight instructor. Most people take more than fifty hours, including ten hours of "cross-country" flying and ten hours of solo flight. Each lesson costs approximately $25 an hour. But you also need thirty hours of ground school in order to pass the required written test. Your health must be reasonably good, with excellent acuity for hearing and seeing. You should be able to hear a whisper from three feet away and distinguish between red, green, and white. If you measure up, you may never have to take a regularly scheduled airline flight again. You'll just swoop down to visit faraway friends on your own schedule. Most of the 130,000 or so people who'll take up flying this year schedule two or three lessons a week and complete the course in four to six months. Ground school covers principles of flight, navigation, meteorology, federal aviation regulations, and medical facts (including hypoxia, hyperventilation, and the effects of rapid descents on closed sinuses). Even when you've earned your pilot's license, you'll still have to be checked out every two years by an instructor—just to prove that your memory is as good as your general health. If you do well, you'll keep on piloting; if you don't do well, the only flying you'll be doing is in the non-smoking section of coach.

Copyright Your Song

When you tell people you've copyrighted your song, somehow that tune has a ring of importance. Actually, getting a copyright is like taking out a small insurance policy—it signifies a need for protection; it does not imply importance or value. Any song writer can do it, and should do it.

When you've finished writing the great American song, alone or with a collaborator, simply write to the Register of Copyrights and ask for Form E. Form E is appropriate for unpublished and published musical compositions by authors who are U.S. citizens or, as the form puts it, "domiciliaries." It is also for musical compositions first published in the United States.

The term "musical composition" includes those consisting of music alone or of words and music combined. It also includes arrangements and other versions of earlier compositions, if new copyrightable work of authorship has been added. Song poems and other works consisting of words without music are not considered "musical compositions." Works of that type are not registerable for copyright in unpublished form.

To obtain copyright registration, mail Form E properly completed and signed to the Register of Copyrights along with one complete copy of the musical composition, and a fee of $6.00. Manuscripts are not returned, so don't include your only copy.

On October 19, 1976, President Ford signed Public Law No. 94-553, the first general revision of the United States copyright law since 1909. The new law, effective January 1, 1978, grants longer protection and greater rights for creators. Works copyrighted before January 1, 1978, will have a total copyright term of seventy-five years—an initial term of twenty-eight years, and a renewal term of forty-seven years.

For works first created or copyrighted after January 1, 1978, the term of copyright will be the life of the author plus fifty years. A work is "created" when it is "fixed in a copy or phonorecord for the first time." The term "author" includes composer and lyricist. And that's all there is to it.

Depending on Lady Luck, your copyright will be either a piece of paper costing $6.00 (and suitable for framing) or your guarantee for a lifetime of royalty checks, and checks for your heirs as well.

Have an Audience with the Pope

As the Pope gets older, he finds time for fewer and fewer audiences. Those he grants fall into four distinct categories: household audiences are meetings the Pope holds with members of the
Vatican community; official audiences are to greet foreign
church officials and government leaders; a general audience accommodates large groups and refers to the Pope's appearances at
St. Peter's; private audiences, arranged for one or two special
people, are vied for by influential individuals of all denomi-
nations.

If you just want to peep at the Pope or possibly say a quick
"Come sta?" to His Holiness, your best bet is to arrange for a
general audience through the Bishop's Office (Rome) for Visitors to the Vatican.

There you will secure passes to St. Peter's furnished weekly by
the Office of Prefecture of the Apostolic Household. Excommu-
nicants need not apply, for you must be *persona grata* to appear
in the Pope's presence. If all this is too much trouble, just stand
outside the Vatican (near the rosary vendors) on any Sunday
morning when the Pope is in town and watch him wave from his
window. Don't count on bumping into him while strolling
through the Sistine Chapel.

If you'd prefer a private audience, you must either occupy a
special place in society—a well-known feminist, a leading opera
star, a shipping tycoon—or secure a letter from an influential
bishop to a high-ranking Vatican official. This is not to say that
if you wish to make a sizable donation to Church coffers such
beneficence might not goad your local cardinal into requesting a
special blessing for you from the Pope, but you'd have to go
about it subtly and drop numerous hints.

If you do wangle a few moments with the Pope, remember to
kiss his ring (if you're Catholic) upon greeting him. Refer to

him as "His Holiness" (in Italian it's *"Sua Santità"*). Don't offer clever conversational gambits and don't be controversial: avoid mentioning your friend's recent abortion or the Crusades. The Pope is rarely alone during private audiences; various monsignors are there, as well as aides to help with translation. To conclude the audience, the Pope most likely will rise, clasp his visitor's hands, and offer a blessing. He may also give you a small gift, like a medal struck at the Vatican—a lasting souvenir of your visit to the Apostolic Palace.

Women are advised to wear a black dress and black head scarf (short sleeves and raised hems are considered gauche); for men, a dark business suit is preferable to a sport shirt and sneakers.

Enter Your Dog in the Westminster Kennel Club Show _____

The Westminster Kennel Club watches over pedigree pooches, and its annual show, held at Madison Square Garden, is the canine social event of the year. It's the longest-running dog show in America, and a great place to walk your dog.

If you think your dog has a touch of class, pick up an entry blank from the Westminster Club and read the requirements for the show. Your dog must have earned at least one championship point at any American Kennel Club-approved dog show. That point is to have been earned at least sixty days prior to the Westminster Show. If you start shaping your dog up now, he might be ready to compete in a year or so and be worthy of the $18 entrance fee required by the Westminster.

In the middle of February about 3,000 dogs are unleashed on Madison Square Garden (actually "lead," not "leash," is the proper word), and the breeds are sorted into six groups: Working Dogs (e.g., huskies and collies), Terriers, Non-Sporting, Sporting, Hound, and Toy. Each day's judging begins early in the morning and continues through late afternoon. Eight rings are used to display the dogs, and they are constantly busy with judges, dogs, owners, and spectators. At night there is group judging in which each dog is judged against others of the same breed. Spectators are welcome to look at—not touch—dogs that are benched in cubicles. Only dogs to be judged that day are benched.

Four winners are selected in each of the six groups. Then the judges decide which of these captivating canines deserves the honor of being judged best in the show. Although standards vary within each breed competition, a few qualities that judges look for are uniform bodily proportion, a clean, shiny coat, and a pleasant temperament. While it's true that every dog has his day, if your puppy snarls at a judge, his day is likely to be severely truncated. He will be expelled from the Garden faster than Adam and Eve were expelled from theirs.

Import Your Own Freshly Smoked Salmon from Nova Scotia

In the barely noticeable town of Tangier, Nova Scotia, is a family who smokes salmon and exports it to salmon fanciers around the world, among them Queen Elizabeth II. The firm of J. Willy Krauch and Sons has been recommended by Craig Claiborne, who deserves a medal just for finding the place (it's about sixty miles east of Halifax on Route 7).

Krauch is a big fish in a little pond, so to speak, but it is to Nova Scotians what Twinings is to tea lovers. A couple of times a week, Willy or one of his several sons maple-smokes a number of freshly caught salmon. The resulting flavor is well worth a trip to Nova Scotia, or the few dollars in postage and duty it will take to bring this delicacy to your door. When that well-wrapped bundle arrives, it will be a joy not unlike your first Christmas. Don't expect the smoked salmon to taste exactly like the Nova or lox you are used to; this salmon will be a good deal

saltier, less fatty, and will have the pungent, sweet flavor of maple blending with all those fishy aromas.

Write Krauch c/o Tangier, Nova Scotia, and he'll send you a list of the varieties of smoked fish he carries. A minimum order of three pounds of salmon is required (less than this, and it really isn't worth the bother). But the price per pound of the salmon is about 20 per cent less than the New York price. Even paying duty and postage of a few dollars shouldn't dampen your spirits when that postman rings your bell carrying your very own side of salmon. You'll have to restrain yourself from having an appetizer of salmon at every meal. When you spring it on your guests, note the envious gleams in their eyes as you detail the smoking of the salmon and its perilous trek to your front door.

Be a Clown

Have you ever dreamed of running away and becoming a clown? If you do want to get paid for clowning around, the place to learn your trade is Clown College, that unique institute sponsored by Ringling Brothers and Barnum & Bailey Circus. Founded in 1968 by Irvin Feld, president of Ringling Brothers, Clown College is a school where clowning is no laughing matter: the competition is rough.

This college's application blank is about five pages long (sample question: When was the last time you cried and why?), and after Clown College receives it, you'll be contacted and told when the circus will be passing through your home town. In each major city of the circus' tour, auditions are held, usually directed by boss clown Frosty Little, to give you an opportunity to strut your stuff. You may be asked to demonstrate a few gags, talk about your make-up, or explain what makes your gags work. You may be called upon to do improvisations—an impression of a lion, a man with a toothache. If you are a juggler, mime, or acrobat, mention that too. Circus clowns are the last vestige of

vaudeville, and they derive from a great European tradition. To be a clown puts you in the same noble occupation as Emmett Kelly, Lou Jacobs, and even comics like Stan Laurel and Buster Keaton.

The best candidates—based on the auditions, applications, and genuine interest of the applicants—will be invited to attend Clown College. You could be one of the lucky fifty or sixty chosen to attend, tuition free, from the approximately 3,500 would-be clowns who apply annually.

Classes begin in September and run for eight weeks. The Clown College's curriculum includes mime, acrobatics, slapstick, juggling, balancing, make-up, costumes, and prop design. Clown College demands of its instructors in-depth lectures and class plans. Few drop out along the way. At the end of the term, Ringling Brothers and Barnum & Bailey Circus hires approximately 50 per cent of the graduating class, but there are other circuses and there is always next year. One girl who works for the circus was overheard at an audition saying, "Well, my boy friend didn't get into Clown College, so I guess he'll go to medical school."

Use the National Archives for Your Research

For most of us, the National Archives in Washington, D.C., is that special, rather unimposing building on Constitution Avenue that houses the original copy of the Declaration of Independence and the Constitution. However, if you were to walk into the building using the entrance on Pennsylvania Avenue, you'd be walking into one of the finest research facilities in America.

Studying at the National Archives sounds as if it should be only for the likes of Alex Haley, Ralph Nader, or Woodward and Bernstein, but you're welcome to do research there as well. Simply walk in the door, sign in at the security desk, and proceed to

Room 200 where you will fill out a simple form. The form assures the Archives that you are over sixteen, that you are who you say you are (show them your Social Security card), and that you have a specific research project involving materials at the Archives.

Once you're admitted, you'll find that the National Archives has something for layman and scholar alike. It contains military service and pension records that will help you find out whether your great-great-grandpa really did see action at Antietam. There are complete records of various federal agencies, records that reflect how these agencies have functioned throughout their history. These particular records are not catalogued by the library: they are filed according to the individual agencies' own systems of filing (this means a lot of work to those who would expect order or logic to aid their fact-finding).

A lot of people come in "off the street" to examine the Archives' ship passengers arrival lists. It's one way to trace your heritage, if your ancestors were part of the great European migration wave of 1880–1910. Also, there are extensive census records for the years 1790–1950, records that Alex Haley studied while writing *Roots*.

Beyond these resources are rooms devoted to cartography, audiovisual material, microfilms, motion pictures, and photography. The National Archives is the repository for the major Arctic and Antarctic expedition records, and houses America's Center for Polar Archives. Not too long ago the Archives acquired the Air Force's files on Project Bluebook, the detailed record of UFO sightings (only the names of the UFO spotters are still kept confidential).

So, the next time you're in Washington, pop in at the Archives. You'll work it neatly into chitchat at your next cocktail party ("Last week, I was doing some work at the National Archives and . . ."), thus giving the impression that you are among the chosen few to peruse our nation's most valued historical documents.

Persuade a College Textbook Publisher to Buy Your Manuscript ⎯⎯⎯⎯⎯⎯⎯⎯⎯

A best-selling textbook is an annuity forever, or almost forever. Unlike books aimed at a general readership, textbooks are written for specific populations of college or secondary school students, and the people who write them do so with the understanding that their books will have a built-in audience. It's a great thrill to write any book, but a special delight to know that your book is being used to teach students, that it is not simply being skimmed but studied and underlined.

Most textbooks show a modest profit for author and publisher, but a best-selling textbook can be a bonanza—not just for a year or two but for decades. Paul Samuelson's ecnomics textbook has sold more than 2,000,000 copies, and I wouldn't even venture a guess at how many art history students have trudged to local college bookstores to purchase Jansen's *History of Art*.

People who write textbooks do so for several possible reasons: it gives them immediate status in their field, earns them brownie points toward tenure, and can earn them enough lucre so that they never have to touch another piece of chalk again. Let's investigate your chances of success.

The first bit of advice is: "Write a textbook for a basic course." After all, your chances of selling a great number of books are better if there are 300,000 students enrolled in a course (nationwide) than if the course is an obscure elective. This way, even if you only capture 10 per cent of the market, you're still doing very, very well. If you're after smaller game, you may face less competition but the financial rewards will be smaller. Still, a book such as Lee's *Oral Interpretation* has captured a 25 per cent market share for almost two decades, reaping a modest but steady income for the now retired author.

To sell your textbook, you must convince a publisher that

you've studied the market, that you have a distinctive approach to the subject, and that you write well. Generally speaking, an editor will ask you to submit several chapters plus an outline for the remainder of the book. He'll then send your material to several reviewers who will comment on its style, content, and chances for success. If you have a terrific idea for a basic book, don't be afraid to submit your proposal and chapters to several companies at once: this adds a certain panache to your manuscript and may goad a quick decision from the usually overly cautious textbook editor.

When you do get an editor on the hook, he'll probably ask you out to lunch and try to pick up your book for the cost of the meal (the prevailing myth is that teachers don't know anything about business or contracts). Bone up on the subject of advances, know the difference between net and gross, and don't sign anything until you show it to a lawyer. And, by all means, order dessert.

Have Your Personal Blend of Pipe Tobacco Registered at Alfred Dunhill of London ─────

When someone says "briars," do you think of vanilla ice cream? If you do, you have no business being in Alfred Dunhill of London, the world's foremost pipe and cigar emporium. This great landmark follows a custom that should warm the hearts of everyone who has ever drawn breath—through a lump of Latakia, that is. For at Alfred Dunhill's—in New York as well as in London—a smoker can register a blend of his own making, record it in a large ledger, and from that day forward order any quantity of the tobacco from Dunhill, no matter where he is at the time. The blend is yours and can be reproduced by simply checking the ledger.

The New York "book" has more than 10,000 blends registered but the one in London has more than 40,000 names, including

those of kings, dukes, earls, and princes. You're ready for the
book when, after having sampled sufficient numbers of ready-
made blends, you are ready to let a clerk aid you in creating the
ideal blend for your own taste. You should have definite ideas
about which tobaccos suit you best, and in what proportion they
should be present in the blend. Try the mixture. If it pleases you,
you're ready to register. If not, try a bowlful of something else.
Once you are registered, rest securely: you will have your tobacco even if you don't light up again for the next fifty years.

Let's create your own personal blend. Perhaps 3 ounces of
Sweet Virginia for mildness. For color and crispness, we'll add ¼
ounce of Latakia. Now we have a cool-burning, flavorful mixture, to which we add ½ ounce perique (from Louisiana) for
added taste. Top if off with ¼ ounce of Dunhill's popular "125
Mixture." Then, in Dunhill's register, it might look like this:

JOHN DOE   No. 66666   3✕5, ½ Per., ¼ Latik., ¼✕125

That's Dunhill parlance for a quarter pound of your mixture, but, in order not to be considered gauche, you should order
at least a half pound of tobacco initially. The most expensive
blend in the New York Dunhill's is a mixture of Gold Blend,
Dark Flake, Royal Yacht, and "3 Year Matured Virginia"
(cured with Jamaica rum)—it costs about $30 a pound. Put that
in your pipe and smoke it. Every bit of it.

ADDRESSES

DISTINCTIONS

Marquis Who's Who
200 East Ohio
Chicago, Illinois 60611

Eleanor Lambert
32 East 57th Street
New York, New York 10022

General Editor
Guinness Superlatives Ltd.
2 Cecil Court, London Road
Enfield, Middlesex, ENGLAND

Cunard Lines
555 Fifth Avenue
New York, New York 10017

Le Cordon Bleu Cooking and
    Pastry School
24 Rue de Champ de Mars
75007 Paris, FRANCE

Director
Federal Bureau of Investigation
Washington, D.C. 20535

Communist Party of the U.S.A.
235 West 23rd Street
New York, New York 10011

Grand Jury
Jury Division Room
100 Centre Street
New York, New York 10013

International Debutantes' Ball
955 Park Avenue
New York, New York 10028

HONORS

U. S. Postal Service
    Headquarters
Washington, D.C. 20260

Académie Française
L'Institut de France
Quai de Conti
Paris 6e, FRANCE

Mann's Chinese Theatre
6925 Hollywood Boulevard
Hollywood, California 90028

National Headquarters
The Honorable Order of
    Kentucky Colonels
The Forest
Anchorage, Kentucky 40223

Department of Army
Office of Superintendent
Arlington National Cemetery
Arlington, Virginia 22211

Republican National Committee
310 First Street S.E.
Washington, D.C. 20003

Democratic National Committee
1625 Massachusetts Avenue N.W.
Washington, D.C. 20036

Miss America Pageant
Atlantic City, New Jersey 08401

Playboy
Playboy Building
919 North Michigan Avenue
Chicago, Illinois 60611

Tournament of Roses
391 South Orange Grove
  Boulevard
Pasadena, California 91105

Phi Beta Kappa
National Office
1811 Q Street
Washington, D.C. 20009

Director of Admissions
Harvard Business School
Soldiers Field
Boston, Massachusetts 02163

United States Military Academy
West Point, New York 10996

Rhodes Scholarship Trust
Wesleyan University
Middletown, Connecticut 06457

Lloyd's of London
Lime Street
London EC3 ENGLAND

The New York Stock Exchange
11 Wall Street
New York, New York 10005

The Palace Restaurant
420 East 59th Street
New York, New York 10022

Central Credit
Las Vegas, Nevada

Dun and Bradstreet
99 Church Street
New York, New York 10013

The Jockey Club
300 Park Avenue
New York, New York 10017

Augusta National Golf Club
2604 Washington Road
Augusta, Georgia 30904

Cincinnati Redlegs
Riverfront Stadium
201 East 2nd Street
Cincinnati, Ohio 45202

Baseball Hall of Fame
Main Street
Cooperstown, New York 13326

Indianapolis Motor Speedway
4790 West 16th Street
Speedway, Indiana 46224

San Francisco Giants
Candlestick Park
San Francisco, California 94134

Miss Rodeo America Contest
c/o Professional Rodeo Cowboys
  Association
2929 West 19th Street
Denver, Colorado 80204

ARTS AND ENTERTAINMENT

Sardi's
234 West 44th Street
New York, New York 10036

Academy of Motion Picture
 Arts and Sciences
8949 Wilshire Boulevard
Beverly Hills, California 90211

Academy of Television
 Arts and Sciences
291 South La Cienega
Beverly Hills, California 90211

American Theatre Wing
681 Fifth Avenue
New York, New York 10022

Actors Equity Association
1500 Broadway
New York, New York 10036

Pulitzer Prize Committee
c/o Columbia University
School of Journalism
116th Street and Broadway
New York, New York 10026

Mardi Gras
c/o Chamber of Commerce
New Orleans, Louisiana 70130

Yousef Karsh
Suite 660, Château Laurier Hotel
Ottawa, CANADA

ASCAP
1 Lincoln Plaza
New York, New York 10023

League of New York Theatres
226 West 47th Street
New York, New York 10036

American Academy and Institute
 of Arts and Letters
633 West 155th Street
New York, New York 10032

The Barnes Foundation
Box 128
Merion Station
Merion, Pennsylvania 19066

Cannes Film Festival
c/o Maurice Bessy,
 Delegate-General
71 Rue du Faubourg St. Honoré
75008 Paris, FRANCE

The Metropolitan Opera
 Association
Lincoln Center
New York, New York 10023

The Tonight Show
NBC Studios
3000 West Alamedas
Burbank, California 91505

CLUBS AND ASSOCIATIONS

The Social Register Association
381 Park Avenue South
New York, New York 10016

The Explorers' Club
46 East 70th Street
New York, New York 10021

The Friars Club
57 East 55th Street
New York, New York 10022

also:

The Friars Club
9900 Santa Monica Boulevard
Beverly Hills, California 90212

The Mayflower Society
4 Winslow Street
Plymouth, Massachusetts 02360

MENSA
Department PK-2
1701 West 3rd Street
Brooklyn, New York 11223

Mormon Tabernacle Choir
50 North Temple East
Salt Lake City, Utah 84103

American Sunbathers Association
810 North Mills Avenue
Orlando, Florida 32803

MISCELLANEOUS

China International Travel
Service (Luxingshe)
Xitan Building
East Changan Street
Peking, PEOPLE'S REPUBLIC
OF CHINA

Liaison Office of the People's
Republic of China
2300 Connecticut Avenue N.W.
Washington, D.C. 20008

St. Patrick's Cathedral
Rectory
460 Madison Avenue
New York, New York 10022

Screen Extras' Guild
3629 Cahuenga Boulevard
Los Angeles, California 90068

Geographical Center of the
United States
Chamber of Commerce (Bel
Fourche, S.D.)
510 South Street
Bel Fourche, South Dakota
57717

A. C. Nielsen Company
375 Patricia Avenue
Dunedin, Florida 33528

Honorary Commissioner of
Patents and Trademarks
U. S. Patent Office
Washington, D.C. 20231

Walter Reed Army Medical
Center
6825 16th Street N.W.
Washington, D.C. 20012

Register of Copyrights
Copyright Office
Library of Congress
Washington, D.C. 20559

Bishop's Office
U. S. Visitors to the Vatican
Via dell'Umilta 30
00187 Rome, ITALY

Westminster Kennel Club
14 East 60th Street
New York, New York 10022

J. W. Krauch and Sons
Tangier, Nova Scotia BOJ 3HO
CANADA

Clown College
c/o Ringling Bros. and
Barnum & Bailey Circus
P. O. Box 1528
Venice, Florida 33595

National Archives and Record
Service
8th Street and Pennsylvania
Avenue
Washington, D.C. 20408

Alfred Dunhill of London
30 Duke Street
London SW1Y ENGLAND